Master the Year 4 SPaG Basics with CGP!

This Question Book from CGP is perfect for introducing pupils aged 8-9 to the essential Year 4 Grammar, Punctuation and Spelling skills.

It's bursting with practice questions to help pupils get to grips with the core SPaG skills, all carefully written to build pupils' confidence.

Each topic starts with helpful examples and there are answers to every question at the back of the book — enjoy!

What CGP is all about

Our sole aim here at CGP is to produce the highest quality books — carefully written, immaculately presented and dangerously close to being funny.

Then we work our socks off to get them out to you — at the cheapest possible prices.

Contents

Grammar

Section 1 – Word Types
Nouns 4
Adjectives 5
Verbs 6
Adverbs 7
Pronouns 8
Articles 10

Section 2 – Clauses and Phrases
Clauses 12
Phrases 15
Noun Phrases 16

Section 3 – Adverbial Phrases
Adverbial Phrases 18
Fronted Adverbials 20

Section 4 – Conjunctions and Prepositions
Conjunctions 22
Prepositions 24

Section 5 – Verb Tenses
Present Tense and Past Tense 26
Using 'ing' verbs in the Present 28
Using 'ing' verbs in the Past 29
The Present Perfect 30
Staying in the Same Tense 32

Section 6 – Standard and Non-Standard English
Verb Agreement 34
Confusing Words 36
Negatives 39

Punctuation

Section 7 – Sentence Punctuation
Capital Letters and Full Stops 40
Question Marks 42
Exclamation Marks 43
Sentence Practice 44

Section 8 – Commas
Commas for Writing Lists 46
Commas to Separate Clauses 48
Comma Practice 50

Section 9 – Apostrophes
Apostrophes for Missing Letters 52
Its and It's 54
Apostrophes for Single Possession 56
Apostrophe Practice 58

Section 10 – Inverted Commas
Punctuating Speech 60
Punctuating Speech with ! or ? 62

Section 11 – Paragraphs and Layout
Paragraphs 64
Headings and Subheadings 67

Contents

Spelling

Section 12 – Prefixes

Prefixes — 'dis' and 'mis' 68
Prefixes — 'in', 'il', 'im' and 'ir' 70
Prefixes — 're', 'anti' and 'auto' 72
Prefixes — 'sub', 'super' and 'inter' 74

Section 13 – Suffixes and Word Endings

Suffixes — Double Letters 76
Suffixes — 'ation' and 'ous' 78
Suffixes — 'ly' 80
Word Endings — 'sure' and 'ture' 82
Word Endings — the 'shun' sound 84
Word Endings — 'gue' and 'que' 86

Section 14 – Confusing Words

The short 'i' sound 88
The short 'u' sound 89
The hard 'c' sound 90
The soft 'c' sound 91
The 'sh' sound 92
The 'ay' sound 93
Plurals 94
Homophones 96

Glossary 99
Answers 101

Published by CGP

Editors: Kelsey Hammond, Catherine Heygate, Becca Lakin, Gabrielle Richardson, Hannah Roscoe
With thanks to Jan Greenway for the copyright research.

The Grammar and Punctuation sections contain public sector information licensed under the Open Government Licence v3.0.
http://www.nationalarchives.gov.uk/doc/open-government-licence/version/3/

ISBN: 978 1 78294 334 7

Clipart from Corel®
Printed by Elanders Ltd, Newcastle upon Tyne.
Based on the classic CGP style created by Richard Parsons.

Text, design, layout and original illustrations © Coordination Group Publications Ltd. (CGP) 2022
All rights reserved.

Photocopying this book is not permitted, even if you have a CLA licence.
Extra copies are available from CGP with next day delivery • 0800 1712 712 • www.cgpbooks.co.uk

Section 1 — Word Types

Nouns

Nouns are words that name things.

Common nouns are everyday words for things. → coat   mountain

France   April   Jupiter ← Proper nouns are names for particular people, places or things.

1) Tick the box next to the phrases where the <u>noun</u> is underlined.

the <u>blue</u> car ☐   for <u>my</u> dog ☐

a slippery <u>fish</u> ☐   an <u>angry</u> elephant ☐

after <u>dinner</u> ☐   perfect <u>pizza</u> ☐

2) Write the <u>nouns</u> on the correct suitcase.

Tip: proper nouns always have a <u>capital letter</u>.

pumpkin

Bristol

January

goats

football

Salima

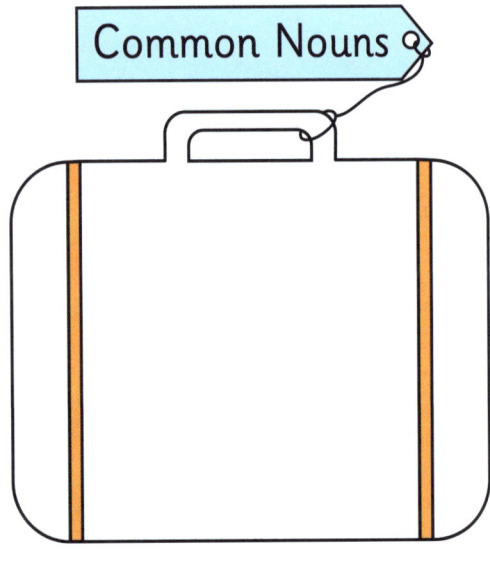

"I know what common and proper nouns are."

Adjectives

Adjectives are words that tell us more about a noun.

a tricky puzzle   the spotty cow   a terrifying tunnel

1) Show which words below are adjectives by drawing lines to the rocket.

explore   adventure   aliens

exciting

spooky

interesting

space

dangerous   galaxies

2) Use a suitable adjective to describe each of the pictures below.

 the .... snail

 the .... bin

 the .... ring

"I know what adjectives are and how to use them."

Section 1 — Word Types

Verbs

Verbs are **doing** or **being** words.

I stroke the hamster.   They play tennis.   She is the boss.

Verbs **change** depending on **who** is doing the action.

We hate sprouts.   He hates sprouts.

1) Show which words below are <u>verbs</u> by drawing lines to the box.

 speak    cake    boat   fun

 pray    learn   Verb    write    see

2) Write the correct form of the <u>verb</u> on the line to match <u>who</u> is doing the action.

I grow potatoes. → He .... potatoes.

She eats pancakes. → We .... pancakes.

They walk slowly. → It .... slowly.

He sleeps peacefully. → I .... peacefully.

"I know what verbs are and how to use them."

Section 1 — Word Types   © CGP — not to be photocopied

Adverbs

Adverbs are words that **describe verbs**.

Julien threw the ball clumsily.

Tip: Adverbs often end with -ly.

They can tell you **how**, **when** and **how often** the verb was done.

She ran quickly. I'll arrive soon. They never smile.

1 Match the words to the labels to show whether they tell you <u>how</u>, <u>when</u> or <u>how often</u> something was done.

quietly   always   later   today   sometimes   nicely

greedily   regularly   now   sneakily   never

2 Complete the sentences below with the <u>adverbs</u> from the box.

tomorrow   angrily   usually

The farmer shook his fist .... at us.

I .... eat my dinner at 5 o'clock.

Diego is going to Spain ....

"I know what adverbs are and how to use them."

Pronouns

Pronouns are words that you use to replace nouns. **This is very repetitive.**

Halina loves rugby and Halina plays rugby every Sunday.

Halina loves rugby and she plays it every Sunday.

This is better. 'she' and 'it' are pronouns.

1) Add the pronouns from the box to the sentences below.

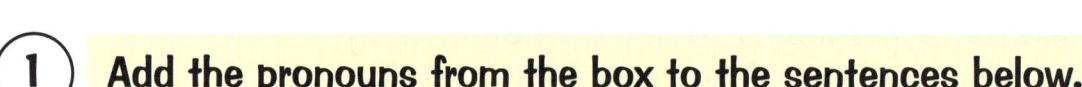

He   They   It   She

.... sing.   .... rings.   .... looks.   .... plays.

2) Complete the sentences using the pronouns below. The pronouns should replace the underlined nouns.

Use each pronoun once.

they   we   them   him

When <u>Owais</u> walks to school, Mia walks with ....

<u>The trainers</u> were smelly, so Anthony put .... outside.

<u>My rabbits</u> love cabbage, but .... don't like lettuce.

<u>Kiah and I</u> were well-behaved, so .... got a treat.

Pronouns can be used across sentences as well.
They make your writing flow better and make it easier to understand.

Alex is seeing his gran today. They are going to the park.

'They' refers back to 'Alex' and 'his gran'.

3 Circle the picture that the underlined pronoun refers to.

Erika loved her cat. <u>She</u> fed it a fish.

'She' refers back to:
the fish   the cat   Erika

Dave ran past the ducks. He gave <u>them</u> some bread.

'Them' refers back to:
the ducks   the bread   Dave

4 Replace the underlined nouns with a pronoun.

The builders made a fence. <u>The builders</u> were proud of it.
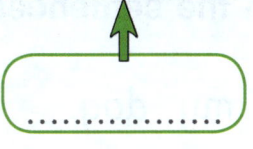

I baked a cake for my sister. She liked <u>the cake</u>.
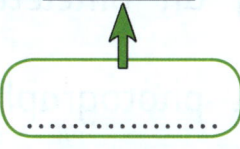

"I know what pronouns are and how to use them."

Articles

Articles are the words 'a', 'an' and 'the'. They go before nouns.
You use 'a' or 'an' for general things and 'the' for specific things.

I have a scooter.   I have the best scooter.

Use 'a' when the noun starts with a consonant sound. → I saw a bird.

I saw an elephant. ← Use 'an' when the noun starts with a vowel sound.

1 Draw lines to match the words to the correct article.

apple   dancer   painting   onion

(a)   (an)

Vowel sounds are usually made by the letters 'a', 'e', 'i', 'o' and 'u'.

aeroplane   exam   toy   bridge

2 Underline the articles in the sentences below.

The fireworks scared my dog.

I am making an omelette for dinner.

Freya took a photograph of our house.

I live in the house next door.

3) Circle the correct article to complete each sentence.

The chicken laid a / <u>an</u> egg in the hay.

I stopped to smell an / <u>the</u> purple flower.

He got an / <u>a</u> bicycle for Christmas.

4) Add the correct noun from the box to each of the sentences below.

> boat   jigsaw   otter

I can't believe we saw an .... at the park.

The .... was painted blue.

Zara asked for a .... for her birthday.

5) Put a tick in the boxes next to the sentences that use articles correctly. Put a cross in the box next to the one that doesn't.

Reece was going on a journey. ☐

I would like an burger for tea. ☐

The cat chased a mouse around the house. ☐

Lindsay found an olive on her pizza. ☐

Write the incorrect sentence correctly on the line.

....

"I know what articles are and how to use them."

Section 2 — Clauses and Phrases

Clauses

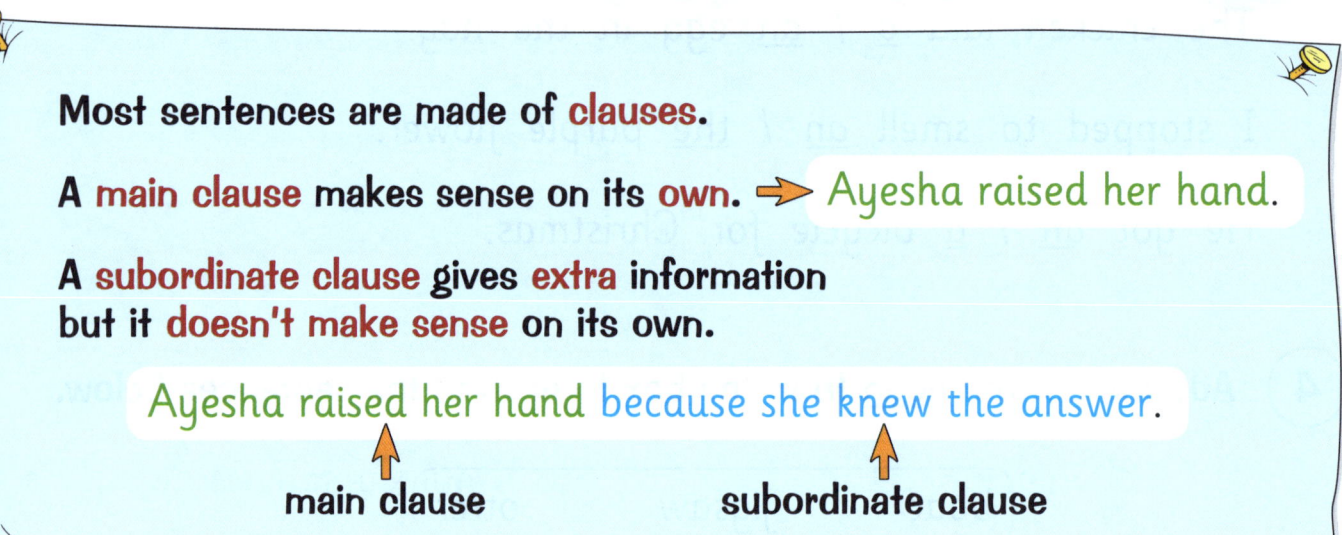

Most sentences are made of clauses.

A main clause makes sense on its own. ➡ Ayesha raised her hand.

A subordinate clause gives extra information but it doesn't make sense on its own.

Ayesha raised her hand because she knew the answer.
⬆ main clause   ⬆ subordinate clause

1) Draw lines to show whether these clauses are <u>main clauses</u> or <u>subordinate clauses</u>.

unless he's busy   who was tall

which was red   — main clause —   if we can

the phone rang   — subordinate clause —   Abel hid

I called them   Annie won

2) Tick the sentences where the <u>main clause</u> is underlined.

The kettle was hot <u>because it had just boiled</u>. ☐

<u>Ali won the contest</u> while Edie came third. ☐

I like to play outside <u>if the weather is sunny</u>. ☐

<u>We shared an ice lolly</u> before we went home. ☐

3 Match each main clause to the correct subordinate clause.

I love art lessons	unless I find my blue one.
Let's play a board game	because I like using clay.
Erin was my best friend	before we watch TV.
I will wear my red hat	until she moved away.

4 Write whether each underlined part below is a main clause or a subordinate clause.

I won't remember the address <u>if I don't write it down</u>.

<u>Although he was tired</u>, he finished his homework before bed.

As the alarm didn't go off, <u>they are running late for school</u>.

<u>We should go home</u> before we get into trouble.

She wants a job building robots <u>when she is older</u>.

5) Underline the subordinate clause in each sentence below.

Meera ate the crisps even though she wasn't hungry.

Although it was late, Andy couldn't fall asleep.

When I am older, I want to be a ballet dancer.

Tyler likes his new house because it has a garden.

6) Tick the boxes next to the subordinate clauses.

unless you are quiet ☐   it's my birthday tomorrow ☐

Bert picked Tia first ☐   although it might rain ☐

because I hate heights ☐   I made a paper aeroplane ☐

Use the subordinate clauses above to complete these sentences.

...., you'll scare the animals.

...., I want to go for a walk.

I don't like flying ....

7) Add a main clause to this sentence. Use the picture to help you.

When it was hungry, ...

....

"I can spot main clauses and subordinate clauses."

Phrases

A **phrase** is usually a group of words **without** a **verb**.

in the woods   really quiet   on time   not at all

1 Connect the groups of words that are <u>phrases</u> to the balloon.

I can ask

despite the warning

in the attic

phrases

really excited

perhaps later

the audience laughs

even though it's snowing

bright red bus

2 Circle the <u>most appropriate</u> phrase to complete the sentence.

Delilah sang — like an angel. / really happy.

Abdul ran — spiky grass. / really fast.

Snakes are — not at all. / dry and scaly.

The owl hooted — soft wings. / at midnight.

"I can spot phrases."

Noun Phrases

A noun phrase is a phrase that acts as a noun.

Noun phrases add extra information to sentences.

lots of rabbits   lots of cute, fluffy rabbits

These are noun phrases. The noun is simply 'rabbits'.

1) Tick the boxes next to the noun phrases where the noun is underlined.

the steep red <u>slide</u> ☐   his <u>extremely</u> fast computer ☐

<u>crispy</u>, burnt toast ☐   purple and yellow <u>flowers</u> ☐

an orange <u>goldfish</u> ☐   my favourite <u>book</u> ☐

crushed <u>ice</u> ☐   <u>a</u> mysterious forest ☐

the <u>wrong</u> jumper ☐   <u>several</u> colouring pencils ☐

2) Connect the groups of words that are noun phrases to the planet.

red light   the roaring lion

they ring   slow down

tall giraffes   *(noun phrase)*   bright green ball

bitter dark chocolate   sparkly purple unicorn

A noun phrase can have adjectives, prepositions and more than one noun.

Prepositions tell you when, where or how something happens.

the grand staircase in the hall
adjective noun preposition noun

3) Put these words into the correct noun phrases below.

Adjectives
yellow   tasty
excited

Prepositions
on   in
with

a crowd of ……………… people

the ……………… car in the driveway

a cup of ……………… hot chocolate

the young girl ……………… the photo

the blue scarf ……………… the red spots

the room ……………… the second floor

4) Fill the gaps in the noun phrases below to match the pictures.

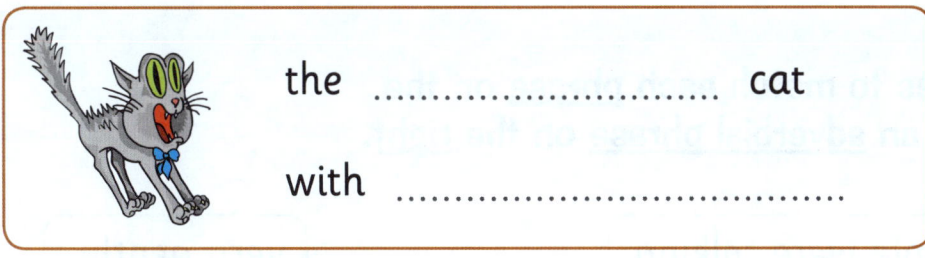

the ……………… cat

with ………………

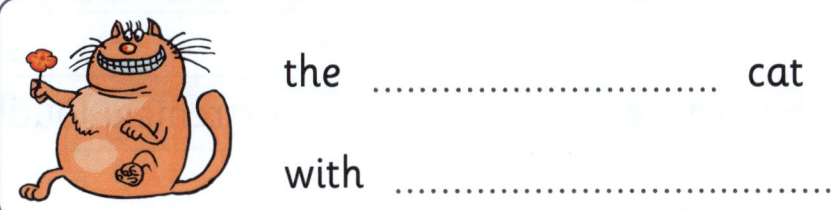

the ……………… cat

with ………………

"I can spot noun phrases."

Section 3 — Adverbial Phrases

Adverbial Phrases

Adverbial phrases are groups of words that act like adverbs.
They tell you how, when, where or how often something happens.

I walked to school quite quickly. ← This describes how the action is done.

1) Circle the five adverbial phrases below. Then write them on the board.

quite carefully

very happily

plenty of sandwiches

too quietly

so badly

really slowly

slow down

an expensive hat

2) Draw lines to match each phrase on the left with an adverbial phrase on the right.

The couple were talking   very gently.

I coloured the picture   extremely loudly.

They stroked the puppy   almost perfectly.

Adverbial phrases don't always contain **adverbs**.

Kay walked for miles around Berlin. ← 'around Berlin' does **not** contain an **adverb**, but it still describes **where** something happened.

3 Tick the <u>correct</u> boxes to show if the <u>underlined</u> phrases are giving information about <u>when</u> or <u>where</u> something happens.

	when	where
My parents organise an egg hunt <u>on Easter Sunday</u>.	✓	
They are setting up a stage <u>in the square</u>.		
We all met up in York <u>two weeks ago</u>.		
Roy and Tabitha always help out <u>at home</u>.		
Fabian's knee started to hurt <u>after the match</u>.		

4 Complete the sentences below using the most likely <u>adverbial phrase</u> from the box.

> quite easily   at the farm
> during the night   every Saturday

Aisha trains with her team ....

I always wake up for a drink ....

We fed the horses ....

Jack won the race ....

"I can use adverbial phrases in a sentence."

Fronted Adverbials

A **fronted adverbial** is an **adverbial phrase** at the **start** of a sentence. You need a **comma** after a fronted adverbial.

After lunch, we went out. ← comma

Last year, I broke my arm. ← comma

1 Tick the sentences that need a <u>comma</u>.

The adverbial phrases have been underlined to help you.

She dreamed of flying <u>all night long</u>. ☐

<u>Before bed</u> he drank a glass of milk. ☐

<u>In front of the building</u> there is a statue. ☐

They danced together <u>under the stars</u>. ☐

<u>Very quietly</u> they left the house. ☐

2 Draw lines to show if the <u>adverbial phrase</u> comes at the <u>start</u> or the <u>end</u> of each sentence.

My dad is going back to work next month.

As quickly as possible, they ran away.

They packed their bags in a hurry.

In four months, my sister will start school.

I found my ring on top of the fridge.

From the window, I saw my rabbit escaping.

Section 3 — Adverbial Phrases

3) **Tick the sentences that use <u>fronted adverbials</u>.**

There is a painting hanging on the wall. ☐

Under the sea, there are lots of different fish. ☐

Over the hill, there is another town. ☐

You'll find an umbrella behind your chair. ☐

4) **Rewrite these sentences with the <u>adverbial</u> phrases at the start.**

[I bumped into my friend] [by the library] [.]

Don't forget to add commas.

....

[There were lots of flowers] [in the meadow] [.]

....

[Chris is going to a concert] [next June] [.]

....

5) **Write your own <u>fronted adverbial</u> to complete this sentence.**

.... , she moves quickly.

"I can use fronted adverbials."

Section 3 — Adverbial Phrases

Section 4 — Conjunctions and Prepositions

Conjunctions

Conjunctions are words or phrases that **join** two parts of a sentence.

We wanted a hamster, but Mum bought us a fish.

first part — conjunction — second part

For, and, nor, but, or, yet and **so** are conjunctions which can join together two **main clauses**. You can remember them as the **FANBOYS** joining words.

For **A**nd **N**or **B**ut **O**r **Y**et **S**o

'nor' is a tricky one. It means 'but neither'.

1 Circle all of the conjunctions.

> nor
> which
> or
> fish
> apple
> for
> yet
> sing
> under

2 Choose the correct conjunction to complete each sentence.

so   but   and

Gopal wasn't feeling well, ... he stayed at home.

She made me a present, ... she got me a card.

They were going to sit outside, ... it started to rain.

Other conjunctions can join a **main clause** to a **subordinate clause**.

Anne brushed her teeth before she went out.

main clause   conjunction   subordinate clause

These conjunctions can also go at the **start** of a sentence.

Before she went out, Anne brushed her teeth.

3   Circle the correct conjunction to complete the sentences below.

Wasim was upset **because** / even if he'd lost his scarf.

After / Although I finished painting, I washed my hands.

It was midnight **when** / until I heard the owl hoot.

Drink some water or / **if** you are thirsty.

4   Join the clauses using the conjunctions below. The first one has been done for you.

I cleaned my room   after   he packed his bags.

Put your gloves on   because   your hands get cold.

I waited outside   while   we stole her biscuits.

She told us off   before   it was very untidy.

"I can use conjunctions to join two clauses together."

Prepositions

Prepositions tell you where or when something happens.

I saw a mouse under a table at the café.

Prepositions can also tell you why things happen.

I was cold because of the snow.

1 Complete the sentences by writing a preposition on the line. Use the pictures to help you.

The books are

.... the shelf.

The sugar is

.... the mug.

2 Draw lines to show whether the underlined preposition tells you when or where something is happening.

There are lots of photos <u>in</u> this magazine.

I went to Kendra's house <u>after</u> school.

He saw the deer <u>near</u> the old mill.

The foal hid <u>behind</u> its mother.

The work has to be finished <u>by</u> tomorrow.

I haven't seen him <u>since</u> last week.

Section 4 — Conjunctions and Prepositions

3) Put a tick next to the sentences where the preposition is underlined.

My sister jumped into <u>the</u> swimming pool. ☐

The plane flew <u>above</u> the clouds. ☐

There was a <u>large</u> forest near the lake. ☐

The children had to be home <u>before</u> teatime. ☐

4) Circle the correct preposition in the sentences below.

I was having fun <u>on</u> / <u>until</u> the slide.

Let's put the flowers <u>outside</u> / <u>in</u> a vase.

The horse galloped <u>under</u> / <u>around</u> the field.

She won't answer her phone <u>since</u> / <u>before</u> 8 o'clock.

5) Choose a preposition to finish each sentence so it describes the picture.

| on | next to | in | under | in front of |

The boy is .... the bench.

The bird is sitting .... the bench.

The bucket is .... the bench.

The sandals are .... the bench.

The ball is .... the boy's hands.

"I can use prepositions correctly in my sentences."

Section 5 — Verb Tenses

Present Tense and Past Tense

Use the simple present tense to write about something that happens regularly.

Rhiannon plays football.

Rhiannon does this regularly, even if she isn't doing it right now.

Use the simple past tense to write about something that's finished.

Ryan washed his clothes.

To make most verbs into the simple past tense, you add 'ed' on the end.

1) Draw lines to match the words to the correct <u>tense</u>.

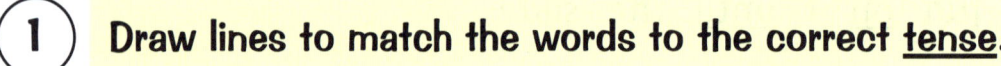

smiled   jumped

scratch   throw

wanted   skipped

shout   hug

simple past

simple present

2) Complete the table by adding the <u>simple present</u> or <u>simple past</u> tense of each verb.

Simple Present Tense	Simple Past Tense
I wait outside.	I .... outside.
He .... to the postman.	He talked to the postman.
She hates peas.	She .... peas.
They .... at the clown.	They laughed at the clown.
We relax at home.	We .... at home.

Section 5 — Verb Tenses

Some irregular verbs are more tricky to change into the simple past tense — you just have to learn these.

I leap back. ➔ I leapt back.   I eat meat. ➔ I ate meat.

3 Shade in the clouds to show the correct <u>simple past tense</u> form of the verbs.

swim

(swimmed) (swam)

ask

(asked) (askt)

bite

(bited) (bit)

kiss

(kissed) (kisst)

4 Complete the sentences using the <u>verbs</u> on the right.

They .... for everyone's meal.

I .... toy models of trains.

Sami saw a mouse and .... loudly.

Yesterday, I .... cricket with Shaun.

Carly .... all the goals for her team.

We .... the bus to school.

buy
paid
scores
take
watched
screamed

"I can use the simple present and simple past tenses."

Using 'ing' verbs in the Present

If you want to write about something that's still happening, use the present form of 'to be' plus the main verb with 'ing' on the end.

am / are / is verb ing

I am chasing the dog.   They are sleeping.   He is grinning.

Most verbs that end in an 'e' lose it before adding 'ing'.

Some verbs that end in a consonant double it before adding 'ing'.

1 Complete the sentences using the present tense verb 'to be' and the words in the box.

cooking   writing   having

 She ………… ………………… a story.

They ………… ………………… a race.

 He ………… ………………… burgers.

2 Use the verbs on the left to complete the sentences in the present tense with the verb 'to be' and 'ing'.

dance ➡ He ………………………………………

jog ➡ We ………………………………………

wait ➡ She ………………………………………

"I can use the present tense with 'ing'."

Using 'ing' verbs in the Past

'ing' verbs in the past are formed like 'ing' verbs in the present.
You just have to put the verb 'to be' in the past tense.

was / were **+** verb **+** ing   Watch out for spelling changes.

He was going out.   I was trying.   They were skipping.

1) Tick the sentences that use the past tense verb 'to be' and 'ing'.

I shopped all day. ☐   She was knitting. ☐

We were cleaning. ☐   He cut lemons. ☐

He was acting. ☐   I was training. ☐

They folded clothes. ☐   They arrived. ☐

2) Write what each person was doing in their picture using the past tense with the verb 'to be' and 'ing'.

Beth   John   The twins

Use the verbs in the box to help you.

Beth ....

John ....

The twins ....

smile   shout   sob

"I can use the past tense with 'ing'."

The Present Perfect

You can use the present perfect to talk about something that happened recently.

Lily has finished.

It is formed from the present tense of 'to have' and the past tense form of the main verb.

I have arrived.

The main verb is usually the same as the normal past tense.

It has turned dark.

1. Show which sentences use the **present perfect** by drawing lines to the fish.

The door has closed.

The baby was crying.

Kim was falling over.

I have signed up.

 present perfect

We have wasted time.

He has washed up.

2. Complete each sentence using the **present perfect form** of the verb in the box.

Remember to use the present tense of 'to have'.

help	I ......have helped...... to paint the shed.
smash	She .... the mirror.
spot	We .... a fox.
boil	He .... the kettle.
win	They .... the match.

Section 5 — Verb Tenses

Some main verbs are **different** in the **present perfect**.

I have flown once.   She has seen him.   It has begun.

Not 'I have flew once'.   Not 'she has saw him'.   Not 'it has began'.

3 Put a <u>tick</u> in the boxes next to the sentences which use the <u>present perfect</u> correctly.

I have runned a race. ☐   They have fixed it. ☐

He has failed his test. ☐   She has gave me a gift. ☐

I have keeped rabbits. ☐   He has ripped the paper. ☐

It has started raining. ☐   I have catched the spider. ☐

4 Use the present tense of '<u>to have</u>' and the correct form of the verb in the box to complete each sentence in the <u>present perfect</u>.

drove / driven   I .... to work today.

grew / grown   My plants .... lots.

took / taken   He .... lots of photos.

speaked / spoken   Fadila .... to her teacher.

5 Rewrite this sentence using the <u>present perfect</u>.

My cat steals the food. ➡ ....

"I can use the present perfect."

Section 5 — Verb Tenses

Staying in the Same Tense

The verbs in a sentence should usually be in the same tense.

This morning, I grilled some sausages, and I fried an egg.

1) Draw lines between the pairs of sentences that are in the same tense.

We are running.   I have looked.   He was dancing.

She has hidden.   She was singing.   They are walking.

2) Tick the sentences where the verbs are all in the same tense.

April cleans her house everyday, so it was very nice. ☐

I bought a pizza, and then I ate it for dinner. ☐

Patrick is washing the plates and he is dusting the shelves. ☐

We play loud music and dance around the living room. ☐

3) Circle the correct form of the underlined verbs in the sentences below.

Richard caught a cold, so he stays / stayed at home.

We are baking a cake because we are having / had a party.

On Sundays, I see my sister, and we play / played tennis.

Section 5 — Verb Tenses

4 Draw lines to make **three sentences** with verbs in the **same tense**.

- Jill waited patiently — while Ria brushes her teeth.
- Jill waits patiently — while Ria is brushing her teeth.
- Jill is waiting patiently — while Ria brushed her teeth.

5 Write the underlined words in the correct tense in the boxes.

I bought a boat and <u>sail</u> it on the lake.

....

They play cricket when it <u>was</u> sunny.

....

Rajan <u>watches</u> TV before he went to bed.

....

6 Rewrite the underlined words so the sentences are in the **same tense**.

I used a pencil because <u>I lose</u> my pen.

I used a pencil because .... my pen.

<u>Bai ran</u> up the pitch and scores a goal.

.... up the pitch and scores a goal.

"I can stay in the right tense in my writing."

Section 5 — Verb Tenses

Section 6 — Standard and Non-Standard English

Verb Agreement

Standard English is the formal type of writing that you should use in your work. It helps make your writing clearer.

In Standard English, the verb agrees with the person or thing doing the action.

Standard English → We **are** ready.

non-Standard English → We **is** ready.

1) Draw lines to match each sentence to the correct form of the verb.

I ? looking for my rucksack.

She ? listening to pop music.

We ? talking about holidays.

They ? watching cartoons.

are

am

is

Tip: two of the sentences match to one of the verbs.

2) Tick the sentences that are written in Standard English.

I am looking forward to the party. ☐

They is coming to visit me next week. ☐

Jan play football every weekend. ☐

Everyone knows what happened. ☐

He have three sisters and one brother. ☐

In Standard English, you need to use the right form of the past tense.

Standard English → I saw her.   I have seen her.

non-Standard English → I seen her.

3 Draw lines to make four sentences written in Standard English.

My parents have — gone to Paris.

Last year, my parents — went to Paris.

At the cinema, Carrie — eaten all the popcorn.

Carrie has already — ate all the popcorn.

4 Choose a word from the fish to complete each sentence in Standard English.

 been  did  went  done

Lucas and I .... to the zoo with some friends.

Put your hand up if you haven't .... the homework.

Dad .... the washing, and he helped Mum make dinner.

My cousins have .... to Ireland recently.

"I can use verbs in Standard English forms."

Confusing Words

In **Standard English**, the **pronouns** have to fit the sentence.
You **can't** say '**me**' does anything. Use '**I**' instead.

I walk the dog.   Faisal and I walk the dog.

not 'Faisal and me'

Don't confuse '**these**' and '**them**'. '**Them**' is a pronoun, and '**these**' points something out.

These fish are shiny.

not 'them fish'

1 Read these sentences then write the <u>name</u> of the person who uses the pronouns '<u>I</u>' and '<u>me</u>' <u>correctly</u>.

Freya — "Me want pizza for dinner."

Curtis — "My mum and me like dancing."

Petra — "I found a hedgehog in the shed."

.... used pronouns correctly in their sentence.

2 Draw lines to show which word completes these sentences in <u>Standard English</u>.

He doesn't want to speak to ❓.

We should ask ❓ what they want.

❓ cupcakes are revolting.

I saw ❓ steal the apples.

Why don't you like ❓ shoes?

In **Standard English**, don't use 'of' when you should use 'have'.

Standard English → You should have told me.

non-Standard English → You should of told me.

3 Draw lines to match each sentence with its <u>Standard English</u> form.

I would of liked to come.   He could have helped us.

He could of helped us.   You would have been bored.

I should not of done it.   I would have liked to come.

You would of been bored.   I should not have done it.

4 Use the words in the clouds to complete the sentences so they are all in <u>Standard English</u>.

Only use each word once.

have   me   of   I

We would .... been happy to see you.

Melissa and .... sit next to each other.

My neighbour's dog has never liked ....

There's a box .... chocolates on the kitchen table.

5 Put a tick in the correct box next to each sentence.

	Standard English	non-Standard English
Nobody could have predicted it.	☐	☐
They told me about them bullies.	☐	☐
I decided to take an umbrella.	☐	☐
Pablo and me made daisy chains.	☐	☐

6 Shade in the sentence that is written in Standard English.

I wear them boots in winter.   I wear these boots in winter.

7 Replace the underlined words with the correct word in Standard English.

Those yoghurts are mine, but <u>them</u> yoghurts are yours.

I wish I could <u>of</u> seen the shooting star.

My cousin asked <u>I</u> to help her make a cake.

"I can use pronouns and 'have' in Standard English."

Section 6 — Standard and Non-Standard English

Negatives

In **Standard English**, only use **one negative** word to make the meaning negative. → There's nothing to see.

Double negatives are **non-Standard English**. → There isn't nothing to see.

'Ain't' is **non-Standard English**. → I ain't happy about it.

① Underline the <u>negative words</u> in each sentence then draw a line to the <u>correct flag</u>. The first one has been done for you.

Standard English

She <u>ain't</u> playing with us.

I spoke to nobody.

There were none left.

They didn't do nothing wrong.

non-Standard English

② Circle the **Standard English** form to complete each sentence.

There wasn't <u>anybody</u> / <u>no one</u> there.

We didn't have <u>nowhere</u> / <u>anywhere</u> to sit.

He doesn't have <u>nothing</u> / <u>anything</u> to say.

I told you I haven't got <u>any</u> / <u>none</u>.

"I can use negative words in Standard English."

Section 7 — Sentence Punctuation

Capital Letters and Full Stops

Sentences always start with a capital letter. You also need capital letters for names of specific people, places and things, and for I.

On Sunday, I am going to see Libby in York.

Sentences usually end with a full stop.

1) Show which words need a capital or lower-case letter by drawing lines to the envelopes.

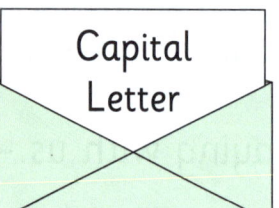

scotland   horse

week   amy

thursday   london

dinner   shirt

2) Tick the box to show if the sentence is missing a full stop or a capital letter.

	Full Stop	Capital Letter
My cousin, jane, has moved house.	☐	☐
I accidentally got on the wrong bus	☐	☐
We painted our living room yellow	☐	☐
i didn't want to go to the park.	☐	☐

3) **Add three full stops where they are needed in the passage below.**

My sister Anya and I are going shopping ☐ We ☐ are catching a train ☐ from the station ☐ I'm looking for ☐ some glittery shoes, ☐ and Anya wants ☐ to buy a stripy dress ☐

4) **Circle the correct version of each word to complete the sentences.**

Yesterday I visited my friend / Friend.

My brother lives near Manchester / manchester.

We / we went to the park in the morning.

I Watched / watched the rugby match.

Today I played with my friend daisy / Daisy.

There's lots to do where / Where they live.

5) **Rewrite the sentences with capital letters and full stops.**

my dog is called barry → ....

sue doesn't like fridays → ....

we are visiting france → ....

"I can use capital letters and full stops."

Question Marks

Questions often begin with words like when, who, what, where or why. Questions always finish with a question mark.

What is that noise?   When will the rain stop?

1) Add full stops or question marks to the sentences below.

What time is the next ferry arriving ☐

We ate all of the cake before the party ☐

Where did you go on Sunday ☐

2) Circle the question words in the box below and add them to the sentences.

Whale	Who
What	Wheat
When	Whack

.... is your friend's name?

.... left the door open?

.... can I go outside?

3) Write a question to match the answer given below.

Q: ....

A: We are going to the Canary Islands.

"I can use question marks correctly."

Section 7 — Sentence Punctuation

Exclamation Marks

You can use exclamation marks at the end of sentences to show strong emotions such as anger or surprise: → This is exciting!

They can also be used to show that something was said loudly. → "Run away quickly!"

1 Complete the sentences with a word from the box, then add exclamation marks to the ones most likely to use them.

potatoes   bed   shark   thunder

Watch out for that ....

I am peeling ....

That .... was terrifying

She is going to ....

2 Write a sentence about the picture which uses an exclamation mark.

scored   goal   I   winning   the

Use the words on the blocks to help you.

....
....

"I can use exclamation marks correctly."

Sentence Practice

Remember that sentences always start with a capital letter, but they can finish with a full stop, a question mark or an exclamation mark.

Carrots are orange.   Where am I?   Come here now!

1) Draw lines to match each sentence to the correct punctuation.

There's a lion over there

Who is she

Where is the shop

I actually scored a goal

I'm so late for school

What's happening

When is the meeting

!   ?

2) Fill in the gaps with words from the box on the left. Then finish each sentence using the correct punctuation from the box on the right.

pizza   hobby   mask   .   ?   !

Yesterday, I saw a dog wearing a .... ☐

Lilith's favourite .... is rowing ☐

How many slices of .... would you like ☐

Section 7 — Sentence Punctuation

3 Write each sentence in the box with its most likely punctuation.

- That's great
- How is the pie
- Why is it dark
- Who are you
- Ouch, my toe
- Wow, how fun

!	?
That's great!	How is the pie?
Ouch, my toe!	Why is it dark?
Wow, how fun!	Who are you?

4 Tick the sentences which use the correct punctuation.

I forgot Ishana's birthday! ✓

Where can i buy some new shoes.

Kit is swimming across the English Channel! ✓

How many days are in july!

Broccoli is a green vegetable. ✓

Tip: There are two wrong sentences.

Rewrite the incorrect sentences below, using the correct punctuation.

....

....

"I can punctuate sentences correctly."

Section 8 — Commas

Commas for Writing Lists

Commas are used to separate items in a list.

> His coat is blue, green, yellow and purple.

You need commas between all the things in the list except the last two. You need to put 'and' or 'or' between the last two things.

1) Tick the sentences which use commas **correctly**. Put a **cross** next to the ones which **don't**.

Have you got any apples, bananas or grapes? ☐

Have you got any apples bananas, or grapes? ☐

The dog, chased a bird, a squirrel, a cat and some cows. ☐

The dog chased a bird, a squirrel, a cat and some cows. ☐

2) Each of these sentences is missing one **comma**. Add one **comma** to each sentence to make it correct.

The jelly could be ☐ orange ☐ lemon ☐ or lime flavour.

Gina's brothers ☐ are called Aidan ☐ Stephen ☐ and Jake.

The journey was long ☐ boring ☐ and ☐ tiring.

Mix the sugar ☐ butter ☐ and eggs ☐ together.

3 Read the lists below, then shade in the correct box to show how many commas are needed in each one.

His mum bakes cookies bread and cakes. ⟶ 1 2

We saw seals dolphins sharks and whales. ⟶ 1 2

I like peas potatoes cabbage and sprouts. ⟶ 1 2

4 Add commas in the correct places in the sentences below.

I'm going to invite Mandy Imran and Sadie.

The house was small dusty and haunted.

The mouse ate the cheese the crackers and the cherries.

5 Write a list that includes the items below.
Remember to use commas in the correct places.

| old brown boots | new rucksack | silver house key | blue woolly hat |

I lost my ....

....

....

"I can use commas to separate items in a list."

Commas to Separate Clauses

You need to put a comma after a subordinate clause when it comes at the beginning of a sentence:

subordinate clause → After I left the concert, I went home.

You don't need a comma when the subordinate clause comes after the main clause:

I went home after I left the concert.

1) Tick the sentences which need a comma.

While he was sitting outside Theo got sunburnt. ☐

If it's raining we won't go to the beach. ☐

The sheep escaped after the fence broke. ☐

The dragon roared when it saw the knight. ☐

Before it went dark Nancy went out for a walk. ☐

2) Each of the sentences is missing one comma. Add one comma to each sentence to make it correct.

Before we forget ☐ let's write ☐ it down.

Wherever ☐ she went ☐ she was admired.

Even if ☐ it's true ☐ I don't believe it.

Because of the snow ☐ the race ☐ was cancelled.

Section 8 — Commas

3 Read these sentences, then write the names of the two people who use commas correctly.

Poppy — Before I played rugby I played football.

Nikolas — If you aren't quiet, I won't be able to sleep.

Aman — I do my homework, while I watch TV.

Rifa — When I was five, my sister was born.

.... and .... used commas correctly.

4 Read the short passage below, then circle the commas that aren't needed.

You need to circle two commas.

When I was in the attic , I found a mysterious box.

I took it downstairs , because I wanted to open it.

After I'd had dinner , I looked inside the box.

I wasn't sure , whether I should tell anyone about it.

Before I re-hid the box , I took what was inside it.

5 The sentence below is missing a comma. Rewrite it and put a comma in the correct place.

If I have time I want to visit Grandma.

....

"I can use commas to separate clauses."

Comma Practice

Remember that commas are used in lists and to separate clauses.

In a list → The troll was tall, smelly and angry.

After a subordinate clause → When I'm at school, Dad walks the dog.

1 Draw a line from each sentence to the correct label to show why a comma is needed.

- The fruit was shiny, juicy and tasty.
- If I'm late, my aunt tells me off.
- As he ran away, they shouted at him.
- I have a rubber, a pen and a pencil.

to separate items in a list

to separate clauses

2 Tick the sentences which are punctuated correctly.

We ordered a burger, some chips and a drink. ☐

Catalina waited outside until they had left. ☐

I hate him, because he was mean to me. ☐

While I'm in town, I will do some shopping. ☐

Should we play tag hide-and-seek or hopscotch? ☐

Section 8 — Commas

3 Add <u>commas</u> in the <u>correct places</u> in the sentences below.

I went to the pet shop to buy a collar a lead a food bowl and some chew toys.

The caretaker asked his boss for a new mop a bigger bucket a better broom and a cup of tea.

4 Tick the box where the <u>comma</u> should go in each sentence. If a sentence <u>doesn't</u> need a comma, shade in the circle.

We danced together ☐ until ☐ it was time to go. ●

If you're lucky ☐ you might ☐ see a deer. ○

Even though ☐ he was tired ☐ he kept running. ○

She couldn't go ☐ because she had to ☐ work. ○

5 Write the items on the <u>table</u> on the lines to complete the <u>list</u> below. Remember to use <u>commas</u> in the correct places.

I put ....

....

.... on the table.

"I can use commas correctly."

Section 9 — Apostrophes

Apostrophes for Missing Letters

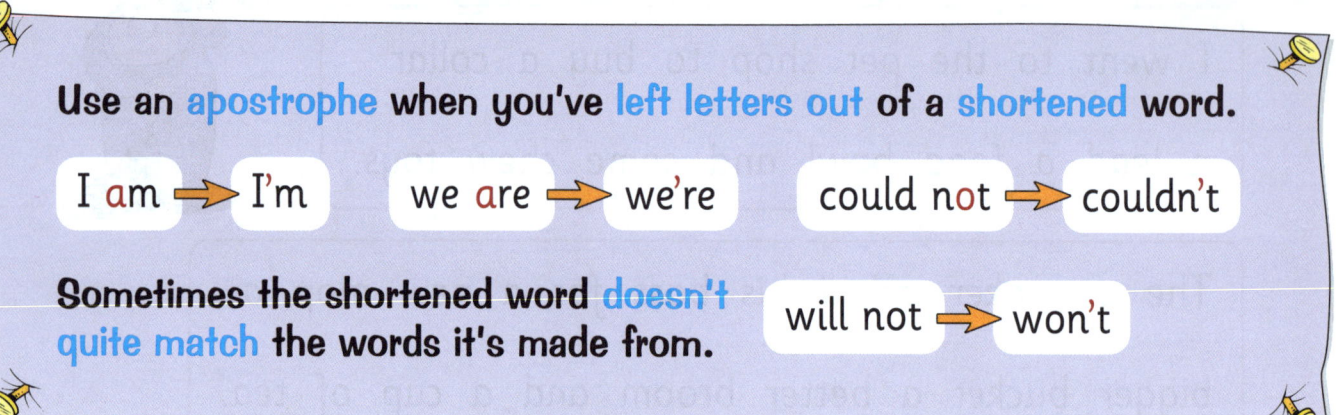

Use an apostrophe when you've left letters out of a shortened word.

I am → I'm   we are → we're   could not → couldn't

Sometimes the shortened word doesn't quite match the words it's made from.

will not → won't

1) Shade in the clouds to show the correct way to shorten the words.

she had — she'd / sh'ed

you have — youv'e / you've

I would — Id' / I'd

we will — we'll / w'ell

2) Combine the two words by shortening them with an apostrophe.

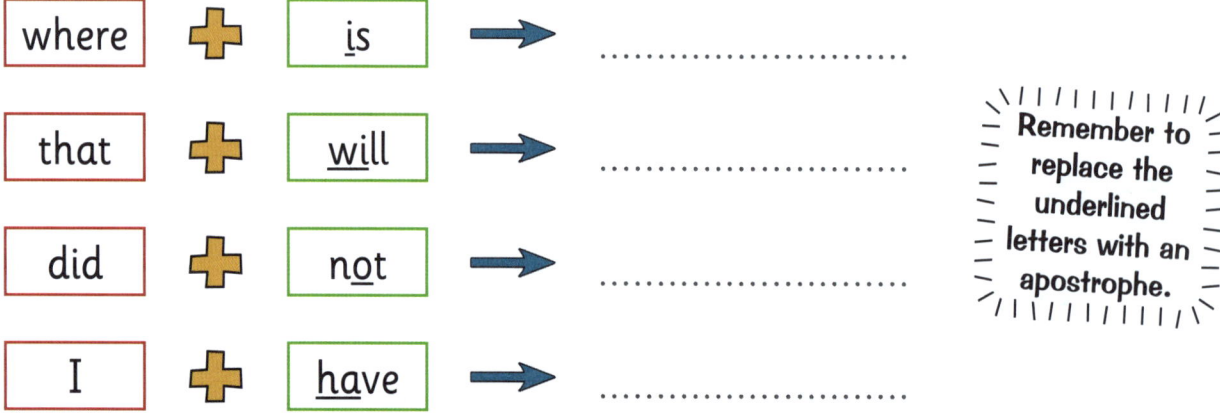

where + is → ....

that + will → ....

did + not → ....

I + have → ....

Remember to replace the underlined letters with an apostrophe.

3) Tick the sentences that have correctly shortened words.

I wasn't ready for school. ☐   We've been skiing. ☐

Hes' in lots of trouble. ☐   They're meeting soon. ☐

Youl'l be tired tomorrow. ☐   W'ed finally arrived. ☐

Write the incorrectly shortened words correctly below.

....

4) Add shortened versions of the words in the boxes to the descriptions. Remember to include an apostrophe in the correct place.

[Sophie is] .... skipping.

[They are] .... melting.

[It is] .... a pencil.

5) Complete the sentences with the shortened words from the box.

[they've   he'd   she's]

My dad thought that .... won the lottery.

Ingrid doesn't eat eggs because .... allergic to them.

I miss my brothers now that .... moved out.

"I can use apostrophes to shorten words."

Its and It's

The words 'its' and 'it's' mean two different things.

its → This means 'belonging to it'. → The dog shook its tail.

it's → This means 'it is' or 'it has'. → It's raining.

1 Draw lines to match the sentences to the correct meaning of 'its' or 'it's'.

The tree lost its leaves.

It's the third time!

It's been a long day.

2 Underline the 'its' in the sentences which should have an apostrophe.

Its scary — it has red eyes and sharp teeth.

I have a racing car, but I've lost its controller.

I don't want to go because its been snowing.

The planet is red and its rings are blue.

Its been in the oven for too long.

Tip: There are three 'its' to underline.

Section 9 — Apostrophes © CGP — not to be photocopied

3) Draw lines to show if the sentences should use 'its' or 'it's'.

... Friday night.   It's   ... name is Sam.

... really unfair.   ... chilly today.

... having a nap.   Its   ... ears are pointy.

4) Write whether the underlined words mean 'it is' or 'it has'.

There's an owl. It's got wings. ....

This is so fun. It's great. ....

I think it's too scary for me. ....

Look at the mess it's made. ....

5) Complete the sentences replacing the words in the boxes with 'its' or 'it's'.

[it is]   I'm going for a walk because .... a nice day.

[it has]   I baked a cake and .... turned out well.

[the bike's]   I can't ride my bike because .... tyre is flat.

"I can use the words 'its' and 'it's' correctly."

Apostrophes for Single Possession

Adding an apostrophe and an 's' shows that someone or something owns something.

the plant's leaf ← This means the leaf belongs to the plant.

If a singular noun already ends in 's', you still need to add an apostrophe and an 's'.

My boss's car. ← This means the car belongs to my boss.

1) Complete the 'Lost and Found' list by filling in the names of who owns which items using an apostrophe and 's'.

Lost and Found

.... bag

.... ball

.... boot

.... book

2) Tick the boxes next to the sentences which use apostrophes to show possession correctly.

Both hamster's are small. ☐   I heard a horses hoove's. ☐

My watch's battery died. ☐   Alena's shoes are pink. ☐

Section 9 — Apostrophes

3) Add an apostrophe to the underlined words to show possession.

I borrowed <u>Deandres</u> coat.

We were amazed by the <u>zebras</u> stripes.

Rosie was the <u>ships</u> captain.

It is <u>Marvins</u> turn to roll the dice.

4) Fill in the gaps in the sentences below. Remember to use an apostrophe and an 's' to show possession.

Jian has a house. It is ……Jian's house…… .

The bus has wheels. They are the …………………… .

The hen has a nest. It is the …………………… .

The fire has sparks. They are the …………………… .

The cactus has spikes. They are the …………………… .

"I can use apostrophes to show something belongs."

Apostrophe Practice

Remember that apostrophes can be used to show where letters are missing from a word, or to show that something belongs.

I'm ← This means 'I am'.

Mo's apple ← An apple belonging to Mo.

1) Draw lines to show why the underlined words need an apostrophe.

Wow, it's spicy!

Chris's feet are huge.

He's laughing loudly.

The shirt's pockets.

missing letter

to show possession

Find Leo's trainers.

Sorry, I'll be late.

It is Sakura's toy.

We're landing soon.

2) Tick the sentences which use apostrophes to show possession correctly.

My cats' name is Enrique. ☐

I peeped into the rhino's enclosure. ☐

The telephone's buttons were broken. ☐

Mias' tea had gone cold. ☐

3) **Rewrite the sentences in the correct box to show what 'it's' means.**

It's bitten me!   It's too early.   It's been hard.
It's February.   It's taken ages.   It's funny.

it is	it has
....	....
....	....
....	....

4) **Rewrite the sentences using shortened versions of the underlined words.**

I <u>can not</u> believe it. → I .... believe it.

<u>They are</u> very pleased. → .... very pleased.

<u>I am</u> shorter than her. → .... shorter than her.

5) **Write a sentence about the picture using apostrophes.**

Tip: Use the words in the box to help you.

| dog   man   sausages   stole |

....

....

"I can use apostrophes correctly."

Section 10 — Inverted Commas

Punctuating Speech

Inverted commas go at the start and end of speech. The first word that is spoken always has a capital letter.

Inverted commas are also called speech marks.

"My name is Alfred," he said.

He said, "My name is Alfred."

1 Circle the inverted commas which are incorrect in the sentences below.

" It's very rainy today, " said " Mrs Griffin.

" Tori is my " best friend, " said Isaac.

" I want pizza for dinner, " said Chang ".

" I don't like maths, " " said Beatrice.

" We're " having fish for dinner, " said Lesley.

2 Tick the sentences that have used inverted commas and capital letters correctly.

"My favourite sport is hockey," said Acacia. ☐

Jamal said, "let's go for a picnic." ☐

"My dog is called Boris," said Fred. ☐

Latoya said, "I'll play outside today." ☐

"We are twin sisters, said Uzoma." ☐

There's always a **punctuation mark** before the **final** speech marks.

Put a **comma** if the sentence **carries on** after the speech.

"They're here," she said. — comma

Use a **full stop** if the sentence **ends** when the **speech ends**.

You also need to add a **comma** before the speech starts.

She said, "They're here." — comma, full stop

3 Draw a line to the punctuation that is missing from each sentence.

comma

"It's my birthday today ☐ " said Ava.

Kieran said, "My birthday is in July ☐ "

Paco said ☐ "I can play guitar."

"My dad plays the drums," said Emilia ☐

full stop

4 Add commas and full stops to the correct places in these sentences.

Lani said ☐ "I want to be a doctor when I grow up ☐ "

"London is my favourite place to visit ☐ " said Oliver ☐

5 Rewrite the sentence below using inverted commas and capital letters.

Nick said, grape juice is my favourite drink.

....

"I can punctuate speech correctly."

Punctuating Speech with ! or ?

Speech can also end with an exclamation mark or a question mark.
It always goes inside the final speech marks.

Jane shouted, "Stop!" Ted asked, "Can you come here?"

capital letter   exclamation mark   capital letter   question mark

The clause that comes after '?' or '!' doesn't need a capital letter.

"Wait!" the woman cried.   "Hurry!" Irene shouted.

lower case   Names still need capital letters.

1) Match the sentences to the missing punctuation mark.

Rania said, "Can you turn the light on ☐ "

"Come here now ☐ " shouted Toby.

"When is your party ☐ " asked Maylin.

Paul shouted, "This is the best day ☐ "

2) Tick the boxes next to the sentences that are punctuated correctly.

Jashan asked, "Why can't I go to Thea's house?" ☐

"It's not fair"! shouted Frida. ☐

"How are you today?" asked Laszlo. ☐

"Don't eat chocolate before dinner!" she cried. ☐

3 Circle the words in the sentences below which are missing capital letters.

Matthew asked, "please can I have some more?"

"get away from the fireplace!" the woman yelled.

Yara shouted, "the zoo is amazing!"

"ready or not, here I come!" Ethan shouted.

4 Put the punctuation from the boxes in the correct part of the sentence.

" ⟶ " What time do the shops open ? asked Karl .

! ⟶ " Football is great " yelled Amir .

, ⟶ The girl asked " Can you pass the salt ? "

. ⟶ " I can't hear you ! " shouted Penelope

? ⟶ " Where is Sabrina today " asked Mr Wilson .

5 Add inverted commas to the correct places in these sentences. Then circle the missing capital letter and join it to the correct triangle.

Kinga thought, which colours should I use?

my team is better than yours! I shouted.

The alien said, take me to your leader.

"I can use exclamation and question marks in speech."

Section 11 — Paragraphs and Layout

Paragraphs

Paragraphs are used to group sentences around the **same theme**.

Start a **new paragraph** for a new **time**, **person** or **subject**.

You should also start a **new paragraph** when **someone new speaks**.

You can show a new paragraph by starting a **new line** and **leaving a space**.

1) Shade the boxes containing <u>true reasons</u> for starting a <u>new paragraph</u>.

- When you're writing about a different time.
- When you're writing about a new person or subject.
- You think it will look nicer.
- When you reach the end of a page.
- When you're writing about a new place.

2) Match the sentences that belong in the <u>same paragraph</u>.

Jonah's father is a baker.	She has broken her foot.
I speak German at home.	He makes pastries.
Amna can't run today.	My mum is from Berlin.
They hated English.	They preferred maths.

③ **Write whether the sentences in the paragraphs below are linked by person or time.**

> Isla wanted to be a mermaid. Her favourite place was by the sea and she loved swimming. She also loved fish but was scared of sharks.

....

> Last year I went on holiday to Spain. I tried lots of food and played on the beach. It was very hot and sunny so I sunburnt my nose.

....

④ **Circle the reason why a new paragraph has been started in the passage below.**

| new person | new subject | new time | someone new speaks |

Our class has twenty students. We are the biggest class in our primary school. I have lots of friends in this class.

Astrid is my friend. She moved from Holland last year. She can speak Dutch and German and is learning English now.

5 Put two paragraph markers (//) in the passage below to show where new paragraphs should start.

Rajesh's birthday is in August. He likes having his birthday in August because he doesn't have to go to school. In July, Rajesh started planning his birthday party. He hoped his parents would let him have a fancy-dress party like his sister. "You're not allowed to copy me!" shouted his sister. He always copied her ideas and she was tired of it.

Circle the reason for starting each new paragraph.

Paragraph 2   —   New person   New time

Paragraph 3   —   New person speaks   New subject

6 Write out the following passage as two paragraphs.

Christmas was Charlie's favourite time of the year. He loved eating all the food. "I hope Dad makes mince pies," he said.

....

....

....

"I know when to break up text into paragraphs."

Headings and Subheadings

Headings and subheadings make a text clearer and easier to read.

Headings tell the reader the main topic of the text.

Subheadings divide up the text into smaller sections.

1 The text below is jumbled up. Number the sections so that they appear in the correct order.

☐ The dog that rescued a cat.

☐ Seb the dog was on his morning walk when he heard cries coming from a well. He looked inside and saw his neighbour's cat, Tilly. Luckily, the well wasn't deep, so he managed to pull Tilly out.

☐ **FRIENDS OR ENEMIES?**

2 Label the heading and subheadings in the text below.

.... → BEST HOLIDAY IDEAS

.... → Paris
The capital of France. Here you can see the famous Eiffel Tower.

.... → London
The capital of the UK. The Queen lives here in Buckingham Palace.

"I understand how to use headings and subheadings."

Section 12 — Prefixes

Prefixes – 'dis' and 'mis'

A **prefix** is a letter or group of letters that can be **added** to the **beginning** of a word to make a **new word**.

'appear' is the root word.

'dis-' is a prefix. → dis- ✚ appear → **dis**appear

The prefixes '**dis-**' and '**mis-**' have **negative** meanings.

not obey → **dis**obey

not use properly → **mis**use

1) Match the words to the correct definitions.

- disagree — to not please someone
- mishear — to not understand correctly
- misunderstand — to not agree with something
- displease — to not hear something correctly

2) Split the words below into prefixes and root words.

dislike → .... ✚ ....

mismatch → .... ✚ ....

misinform → .... ✚ ....

disorder → .... ✚ ....

3) Shade the words with the correct prefixes.

4) Draw lines from the prefixes to the correct root words. Then write the completed words in the box.

If the root word starts with 's', there will be a double letter.

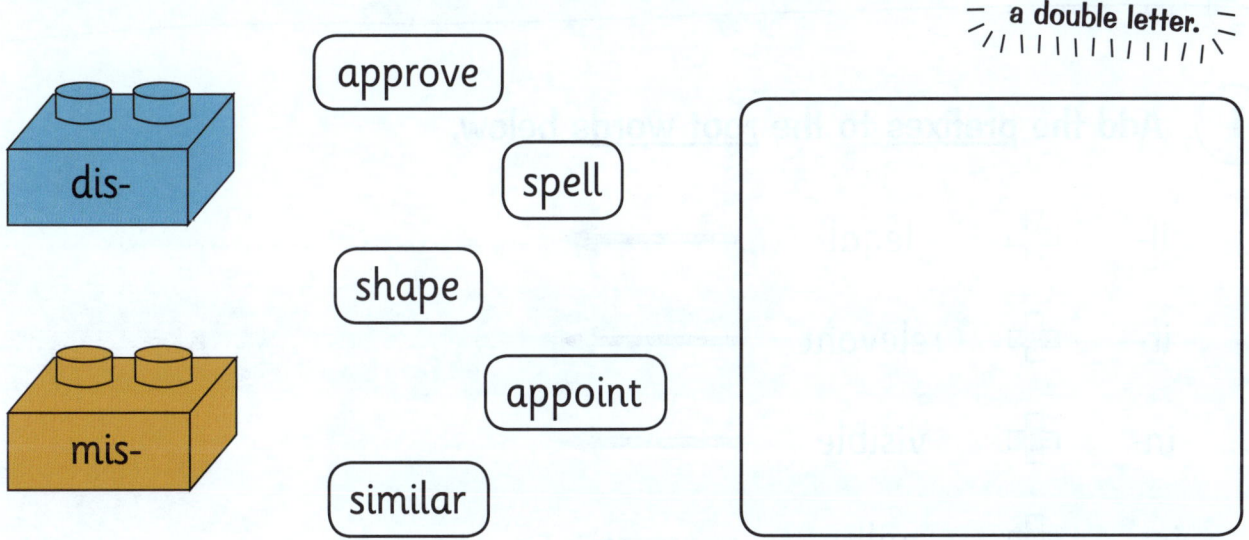

5) Choose the correct spelling of the words in the box below. Then choose the correct word to complete the sentences.

dismissed / mismissed   misprinted / disprinted

They .... Della's picture in the book.

"Class ....," said the teacher.

Prefixes – 'in', 'il', 'im' and 'ir'

The prefix 'in-' means 'not' when you add it to a root word.

inactive ⟵ 'inactive' means 'not active'

The prefix 'in-' sometimes changes depending on the first letter of the root word.

illegitimate   immature   irremovable

A root word beginning with 'l' changes 'in-' to 'il-'.

A root word beginning with 'm', 'p', or 'b' changes 'in-' to 'im-'.

A root word beginning with 'r' changes 'in-' to 'ir-'.

1 Add the **prefixes** to the **root words** below.

il- + legal ⟶ ....

ir- + relevant ⟶ ....

in- + visible ⟶ ....

im- + polite ⟶ ....

2 Tick the three words that will **change** the prefix '**in-**' to '**im-**'. Then write the completed '**im-**' words on the lines below.

correct ☐   direct ☐   pure ☐

mobile ☐   mortal ☐   accurate ☐

....

③ **Circle the words below which use the prefix 'in-'. Then write the completed 'in-' words on the board.**

perfect, resistible, press, expensive, secure, valid, formal

④ **Circle the correct spelling of each word to complete the sentences.**

I have an ilrational / irrational fear of butterflies.

Eating dessert first is illogical / irlogical.

The shape was ilregular / irregular.

Someone who can't read is illiterate / irliterate.

⑤ **Use the clues and the letters in the boxes to find words beginning with 'in-', 'il-', or 'im-'. Write the words on the lines.**

not capable → b n c i p a a l e → ....

not possible → l e p s m i s i o b → ....

not legible → i l i e b l e l g → ....

Prefixes – 're', 'anti' and 'auto'

The prefix 're-' means 'again' or 'back' when you add it to a root word.

remarry ⟶ 'remarry' means 'to marry again'

'anti' means 'not' or 'against' ⟶ antivirus

'auto' means 'self', 'own' or 'automatic' ⟶ autofocus

1 Draw lines from the prefixes to the correct root words. Then write the completed words in the box.

re-

anti-

action
climax
send
clockwise
open
view

2 Circle the words that can be added to 'auto-' to make new words. Then write the completed words on the lines.

graph   turn

build   pilot

....

....

Section 12 — Prefixes

③ **Shade the word from each line which will make a new word when added to the prefix in the balloon.**

re- | body | fresh | venom

anti- | pair | make | bacterial

auto- | correct | social | new

④ **Complete the words in these sentences using 're-', 'anti-' or 'auto-'.**

The magician made the missing rabbit …………… appear.

Dr Williams started to write his …………… biography.

She put some …………… septic cream on my finger.

⑤ **Use the clues to work out the words below using 're-', 'anti-' or 'auto-'.**

not sociable → a | n | | | s | | c | i | | l

| | | p | a | y ← play again

a car → | | u | t | | m | | b | i | | e

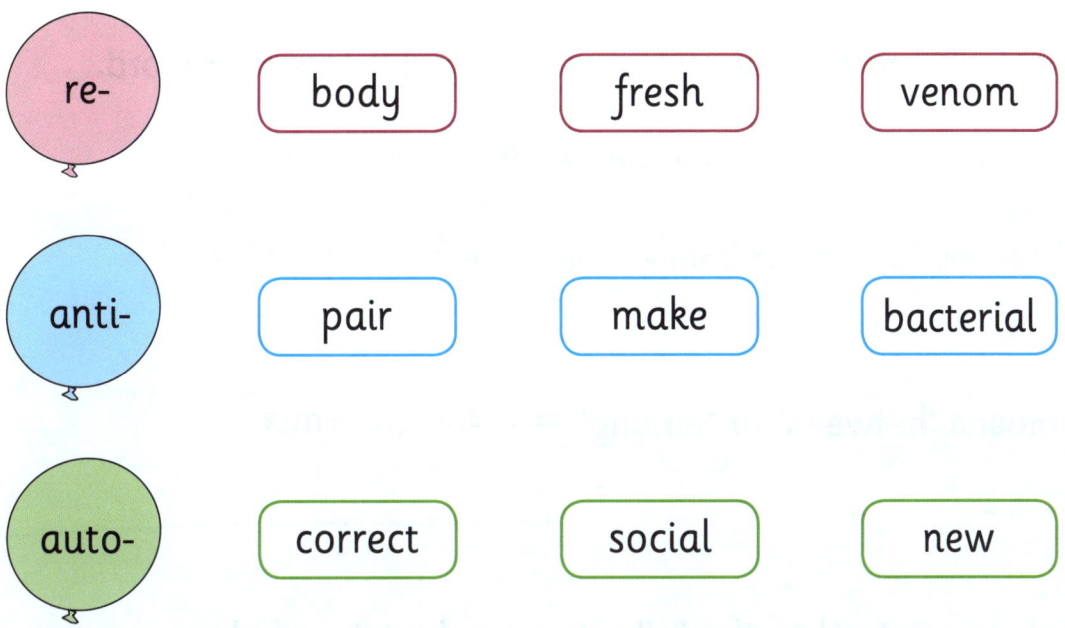
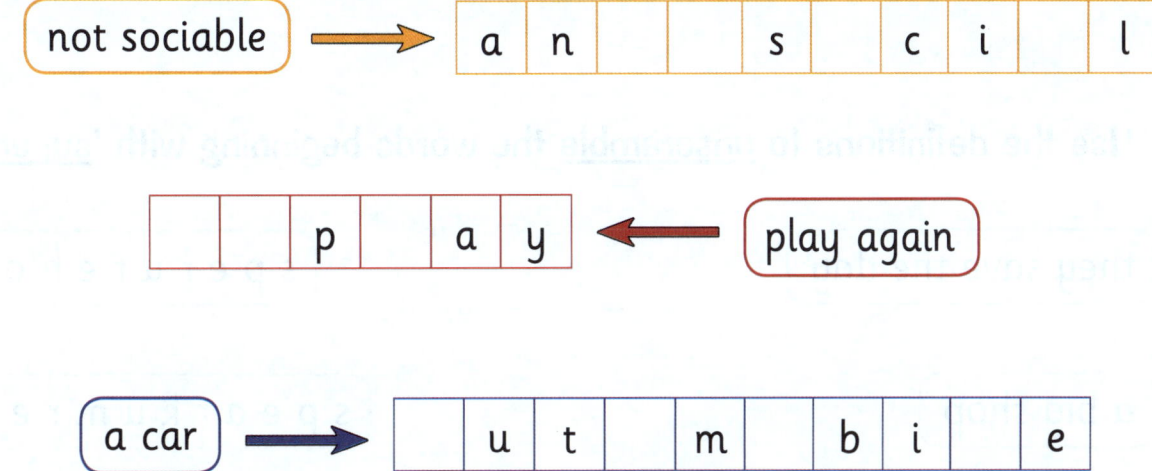

Prefixes – 'sub', 'super' and 'inter'

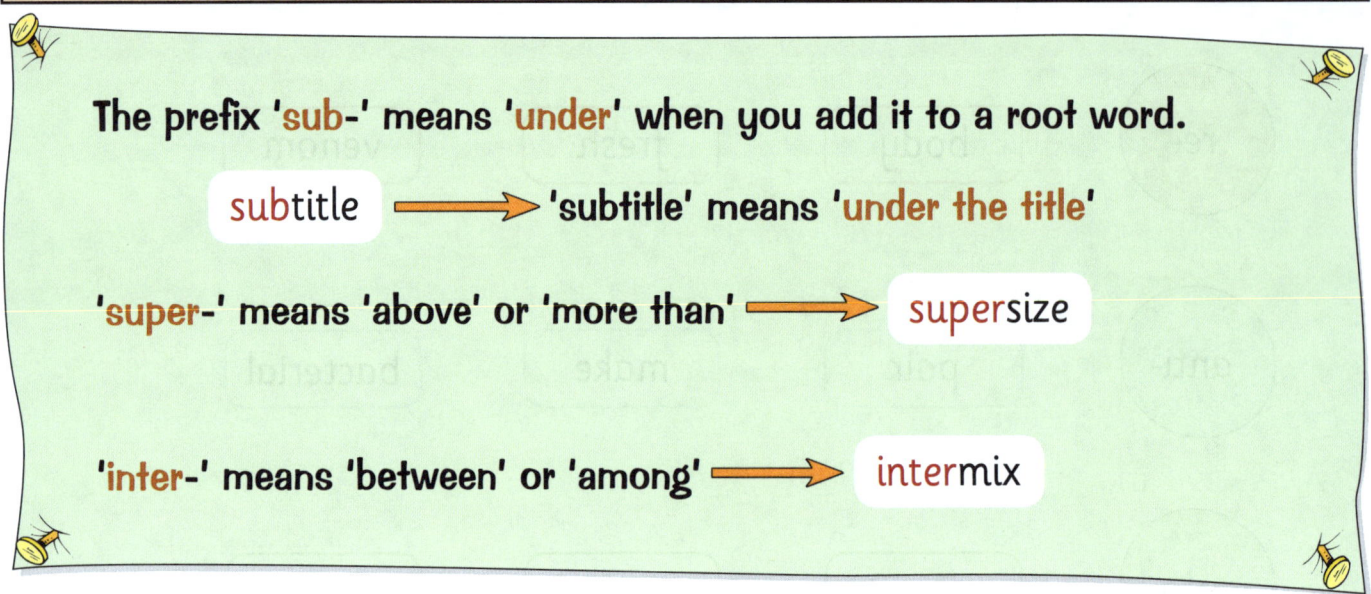

The prefix 'sub-' means 'under' when you add it to a root word.

subtitle → 'subtitle' means 'under the title'

'super-' means 'above' or 'more than' → supersize

'inter-' means 'between' or 'among' → intermix

1 Add 'sub-' or 'inter-' to the following word endings below. Write the completed words on the correct board.

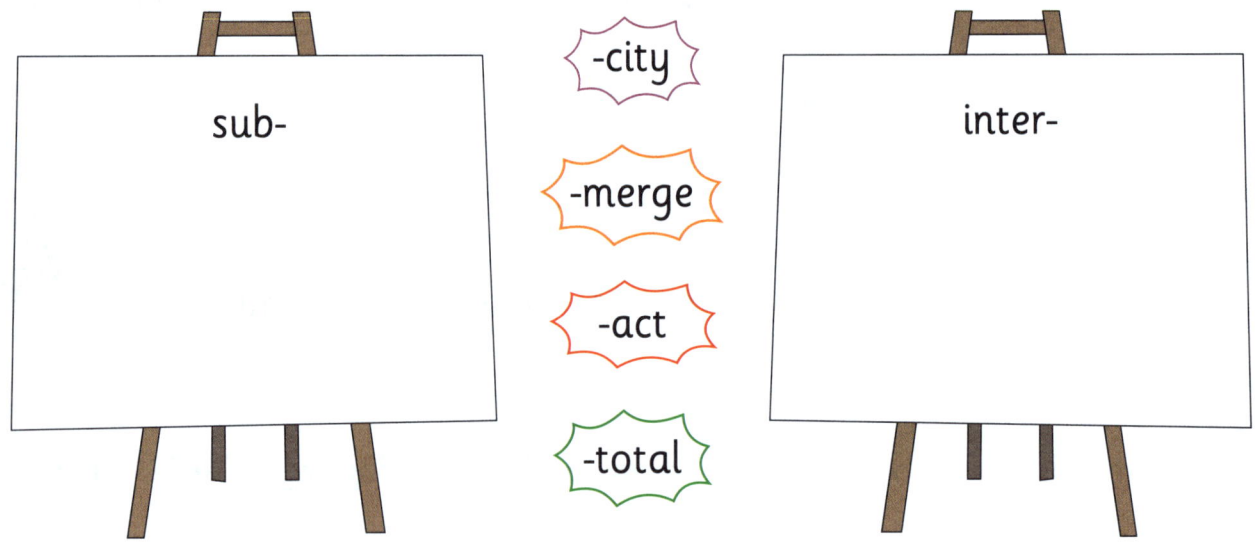

sub-   inter-

-city   -merge   -act   -total

2 Use the definitions to unscramble the words beginning with 'super-'.

they save the day .... s p e r u r e h o

a big shop .... s p e a r k u m r e t

Section 12 — Prefixes

3) Complete the words below using 'sub-', 'super-' or 'inter-'.

The ....way goes under the main road.

The museum has an ....active dinosaur exhibit.

Everyone wanted an autograph from the ....star.

A really big shop is called a ....store.

4) Solve the clues to complete the crossword.

Across
2. You use this to look things up on a computer.
4. below a heading
5. A ship which can travel underwater.

Down
1. a special ability (like flying)
3. very sticky glue

Hint — fill in the prefixes first if you get stuck.

Crossword answers shown:
- 1 down: s _ _ _ p _ _ _ _ _ w _
- 2 across: _ n _ e _ n _ t
- 3 down: s _ p _ _ _ g _ u _
- 4 across: s _ _ h _ a _
- 5 across: s _ b m _ r _ n _

Section 13 — Suffixes and Word Endings

Suffixes – Double Letters

A **suffix** is a letter or group of letters that can be **added** to the end of a word to make a **new word**.
When you add a **suffix** to some words you have to **double** the last **letter**.

'begin' is the **root word** → begin + -ing → begin**n**ing

'-ing' is a **suffix**   The 'n' is doubled.

1) Match the root word to the correct suffix. Then write the completed words on the case.

- grinn-
- soon-   -er
- regrett-
- sharp-   -ing
- cancell-

2) Tick the six root words that need double letters before the suffix '-ed'.

- shop ☐
- hunt ☐
- spot ☐
- garden ☐
- prefer ☐
- heat ☐
- slip ☐
- chat ☐
- drum ☐

③ **Add double letters before the suffixes below. Then write out the completed word.**

hot + ... + -er → ....

plan + ... + -ed → ....

pop + ... + -ing → ....

④ **Underline the words spelt correctly in the word pairs below.**

tripped / triped

singing / singging

lower / lowwer

upper / uper

swiming / swimming

⑤ **Add the correct suffixes to the sentences below. You will need to add double letters first.**

Only use each suffix once.

-er   -ed   -ing

The run.......... approached the track.

The rabbit was hop.......... across the field.

Mary jab.......... her brother with a pencil.

Suffixes – 'ation' and 'ous'

For some words you don't need to change the spelling of the root word when you add the suffixes '-ation' and '-ous'.

inform + -ation → information

Sometimes the spelling of the root word changes when you add '-ation' and '-ous'. — the 'e' in 'fame' disappears.

fame + -ous → famous

1) Add '-ation' or '-ous' to the sentences below so that they make sense.

Scotland is a very mountain............ country.

Many species of frog are poison............ .

Elliot needed rest and relax............ .

Rosa Parks was very courage............ .

My bananas are grown on a plant............ .

2) Circle the correct spelling of each word to complete these sentences.

She tried to find the treasure's locatetion / location .

Peter made preparations / prepareation for the journey.

Not wearing a seatbelt is dangerous / dangeration.

Ayo made a donation / donatetion to a local charity.

③ **Add either '-ation' or '-ous' to the words below. Remember that the root words will need to change when the suffix is added.**

adore ➕ -ation ➡ ....

nerve ➕ -ous ➡ ....

invite ➕ -ation ➡ ....

④ **Add the suffix '-ation' to the root words below. Write the completed word in the correct column in the table.**

sense

expect

create

decorate

form

inform

changed	unchanged

⑤ **Tick the words that are spelt correctly and cross the words that are spelt incorrectly. Rewrite the incorrect words correctly on the lines.**

joyous ☐   fameous ☐   hazardous ☐

continuous ☐   outragous ☐   ridiculeous ☐

....

Section 13 — Suffixes and Word Endings

Suffixes – 'ly'

For some words you don't need to change the spelling of the root word when you add the suffix '-ly'.

final + -ly → finally

Sometimes the spelling of the root word changes when you add '-ly'.

simple + -ly → simply — the 'e' in 'simple' disappears.

1 Draw lines to show which of the root words have changed and which ones haven't changed.

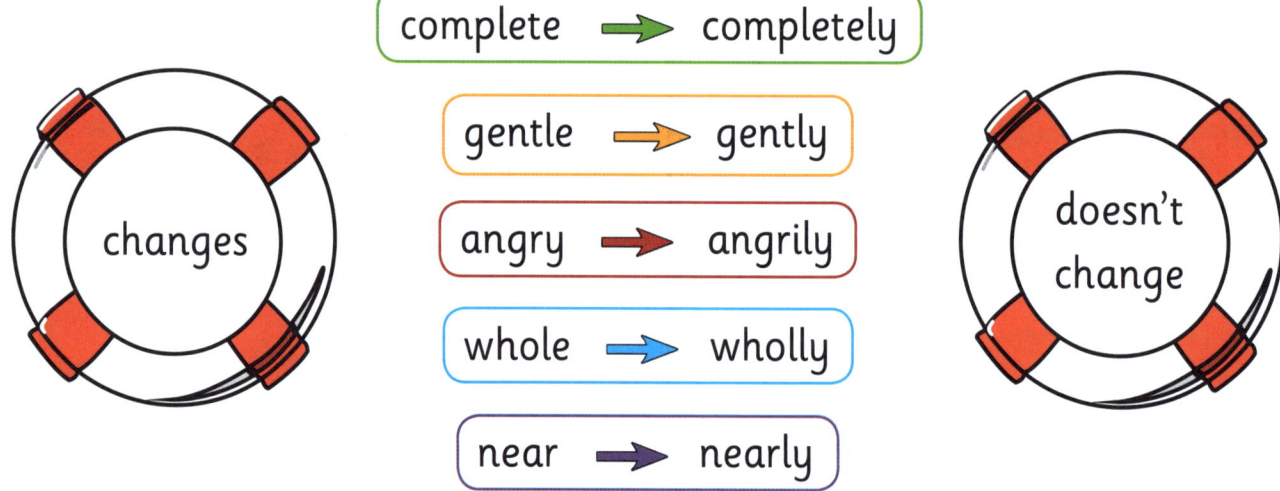

complete → completely
gentle → gently
angry → angrily
whole → wholly
near → nearly

changes | doesn't change

2 Rewrite each word below with an '-ly' ending.

dead + -ly → ....

actual + -ly → ....

like + -ly → ....

Section 13 — Suffixes and Word Endings © CGP — not to be photocopied

3 Draw lines from the root words to the correct words ending in '-ly' in the books.

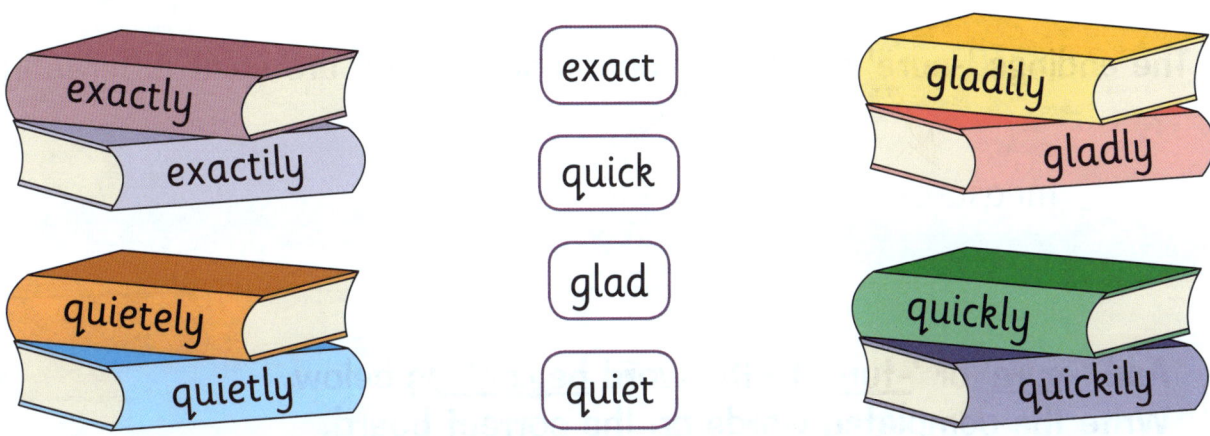

4 Complete the sentences with the correct words from the box.

> easily / easyly   normaly / normally   slightly / slightally

July was .... cooler than June.

The shop .... opened at nine o'clock.

Savannah climbed the mountain ....

5 Solve the clues to complete the crossword.

Across

1. done without mistakes

4. made of wool

Down

2. not roughly

3. expensive

If you get stuck, fill in the suffixes first.

Word Endings – 'sure' and 'ture'

The endings '-sure' and '-ture' sound similar, but are spelt differently.

measure   picture

1) Add '-sure' or '-ture' to the word beginnings below. Write the completed words on the correct board.

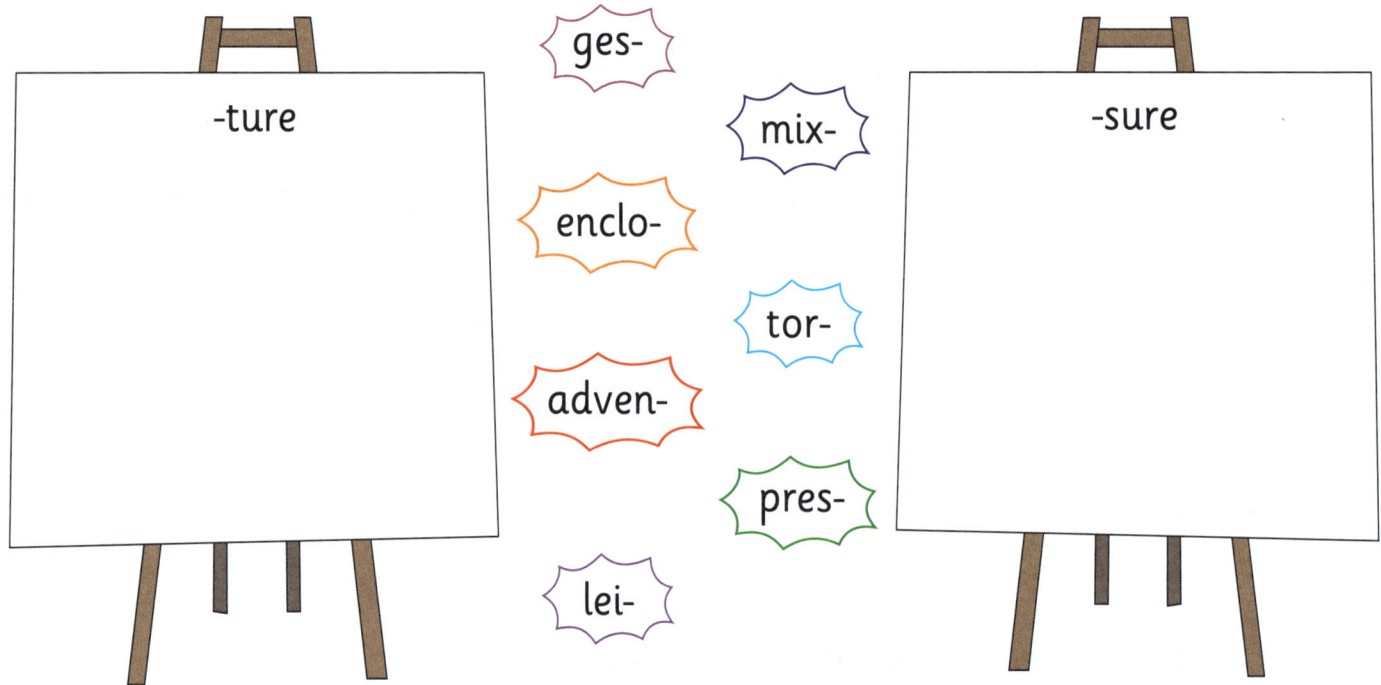

2) Circle the correct spelling of each word to complete the sentences.

There was a lot of moisture / moissure in the air.

"It's my pleature / pleasure to be here," he said.

A factory was built to manufacsure / manufacture cars.

The creature / creasure growled as I approached the cage.

③ **Unscramble** the letters and use the **pictures** to work out the words ending in '**-sure**' or '**-ture**' below.

t _ _ _ _ _ _ _

n _ _ _ _ _ _

f _ _ _ _ _ _ _ _

④ Add '**-sure**' or '**-ture**' to spell the words **correctly**.

litera- ➕ .... ➡ ....

mea- ➕ .... ➡ ....

struc- ➕ .... ➡ ....

⑤ Add '**-sure**' or '**-ture**' to the sentences below so that they make sense.

Thermometers record the tempera.............. of something.

The clo.............. of the village shop angered the locals.

My grandpa loves making minia.............. models of ships.

Word Endings – the 'shun' sound

When it comes at the end of words, the 'shun' sound can be spelt in different ways.

Careful — there are some exceptions to these rules.

relate → relation

music → musician

'-tion' is usually used when the root word ends in 't' or 'te'.

'-cian' is used when the root word ends in 'c' or 'cs'.

1 Tick the words that end correctly and cross the words that don't. Write the correct spellings of the incorrect words on the lines.

location ☐   accian ☐   ....

politician ☐   suggestion ☐   ....

invencian ☐   electrition ☐   ....

2 Complete the sentences using the correct words from the box below.

injection / injeccian   optician / optition

magition / magician

The doctor gave the baby her ....

The .... turned the prince into a frog.

Gloria went to the .... for an eye test.

Section 13 — Suffixes and Word Endings

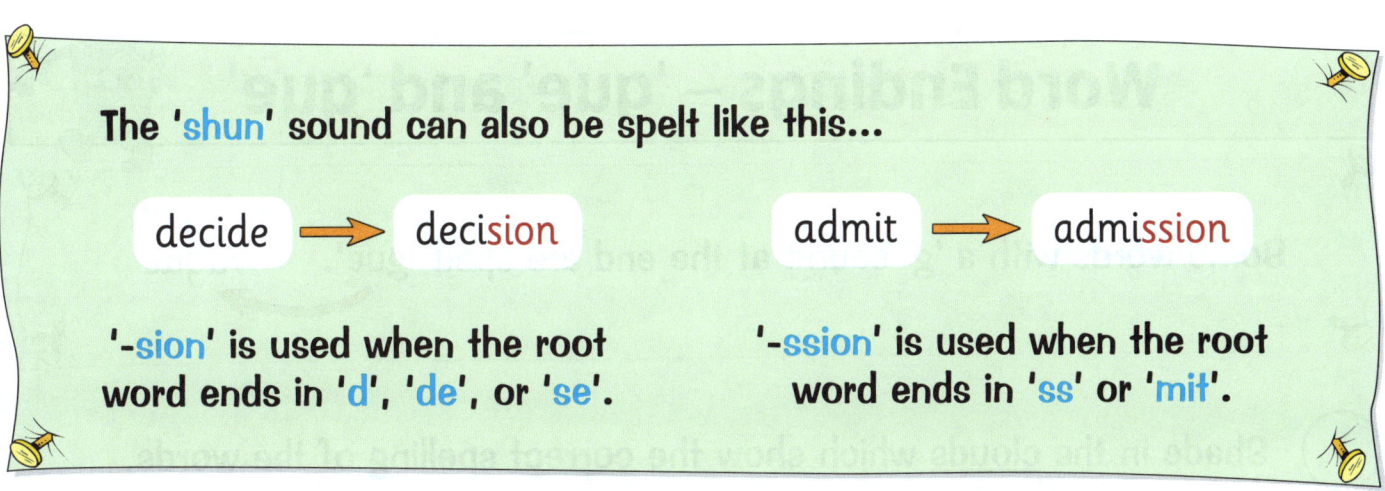

③ Match the correct word ending to the word beginnings below. Write the completed words in the correct column on the board.

④ Add the correct word endings to complete the words in the passage below.

Only use each word ending once.

The mathemati………. is great with numbers. She is especially good at divi………. and can find a solu………. to any maths problem. She runs a weekly se………. at her local school.

Word Endings – 'gue' and 'que'

Some words with a 'g' sound at the end are spelt 'gue'. → vague

1 Shade in the clouds which show the correct spelling of the words.

2 Add 'g' or 'gue' to the sentences below so that they make sense.

She looked through the catalo............ for a new fridge.

The birds started to sing their morning son............ .

The boy's ton............ got stuck to his ice lolly.

3 Use the clue to work out the word ending in 'gue'.

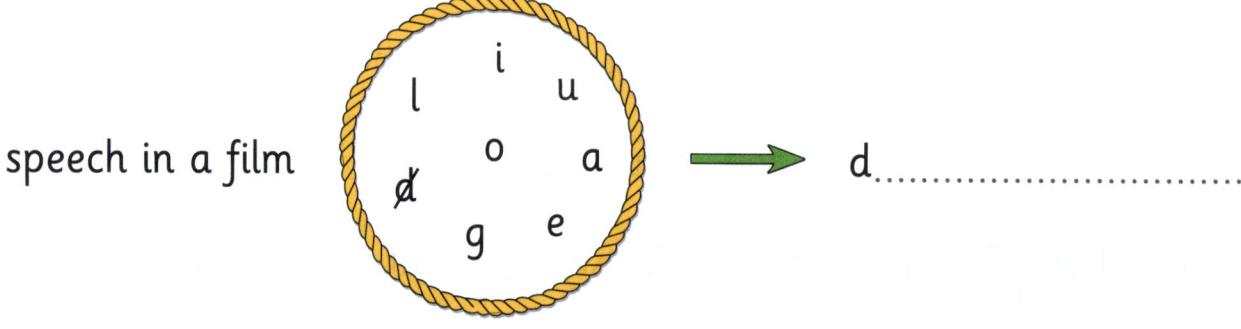

speech in a film → d...............................

Some words with a 'k' sound at the end are spelt 'que'. → unique

4) Draw lines to the correct word ending for each word.

Stars: pla-, bouti-, ban-, tas-, grotes-, mos-
Rockets: k, que

5) Circle the correct spelling of each word to complete the sentences.

The tiger stalqued / stalked its prey.

They tried to learn the technik / technique.

The lizard basked / basqued in the sun.

She took a chunque / chunk of cheese.

I brought two flasks / flasques of tea.

6) Use the clue to work out the word ending in 'que'.

n ~~a~~ i u e t q → | a | | | | | |

something old and valuable

Section 14 — Confusing Words

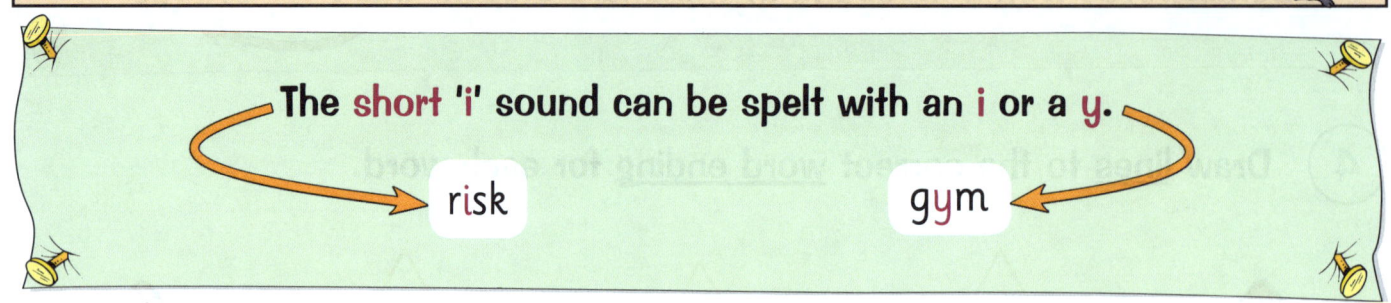

The short 'i' sound

The short 'i' sound can be spelt with an **i** or a **y**.

risk   gym

1) Circle the words that are spelt correctly.

blyss / bliss   ginger / gynger   typtoe / tiptoe

Egipt / Egypt   lyst / list

2) The short 'i' sounds from the words below are missing. Draw lines to match each word to the correct missing letter.

s?ster   b?tter

l?zard   i   m?stery

p?ramid   s?gnal

v?ctory   y   s?stem

3) Complete the sentences below using the correct words from the box.

discover / dyscover   bicicle / bicycle

The astronaut hoped to .... a new planet.

I rode my .... to school on Monday.

The short 'u' sound

The short 'u' sound can be spelt in several different ways.

d**ou**ble   m**o**ther   **u**ntie

1 Circle the correct spelling of each word to complete the sentences below.

My brother / brouther plays basketball.

These gluves / gloves belong to Nala.

The car was old and rousty / rusty.

2 Fill in the missing letters to complete each word correctly. All the words have the short 'u' sound. Use the pictures to help you.

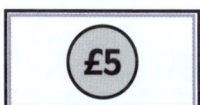
m……ney

f……nfair

tr……ble

3 Unscramble the letters to make two words with the short 'u' sound. Use the clues to help you.

the first day of the week

| M | | d | | |

the sound that follows lightning

| t | | | n | d | |

The hard 'c' sound

The hard 'c' sound is like a 'k' sound. It can be spelt several different ways.

du**ck**   **s**kirt   mani**c**   **s**chool

1 Write the correct spelling of the hard 'c' sound to match each of the pictures below. Write your answers on the dotted lines.

boo**ck**   tal**c**ing   picni**k**

....

2 Complete the words with a hard 'c' sound. Use the pictures to help you.

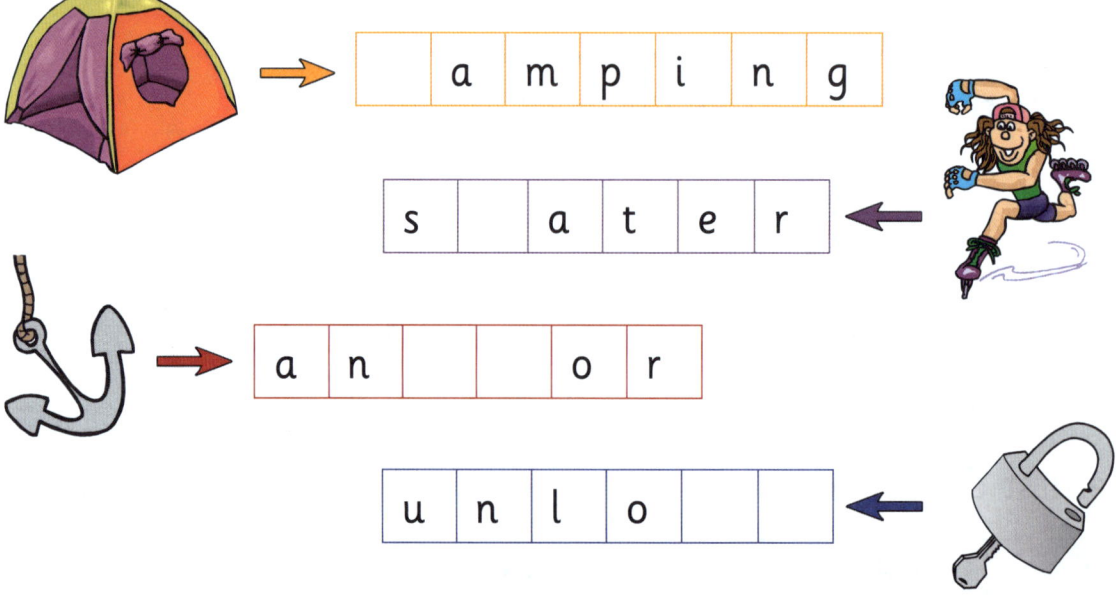

| | a | m | p | i | n | g |

| s | | a | t | e | r |

| a | n | | o | r |

| u | n | l | o | | |

Section 14 — Confusing Words

The soft 'c' sound

The soft 'c' sound is like an 's' sound. It can be spelt several different ways.

scene   rice

1) Shade in the clouds which show the correct spelling of the words.

sentury century

fleece fleesce

pase pace

police polise

peasce peace

concert consert

2) Read each sentence, then write the name of the person who has spelt the underlined word correctly.

Ophelia — Sience is my favourite subject at school.

Gethin — There are some mice living in the house.

Douglas — Can anyone lend me a penscil?

.... has spelt the underlined word correctly.

3) Complete the sentences with the correct spelling of the soft 'c' sound.

Nobody in the offi..........e ate any cake.

Lina collected the par.........el on her way home.

I used some ....issors to cut out the shapes.

The 'sh' sound

The 'sh' sound can be spelt in several different ways.

sheep   brochure   sure

1 Shade in all the words that are spelt correctly.

finish   squach   tissue   mached   shiver

2 Fill in the missing letters to complete each word correctly. All the words have the 'sh' sound. Use the pictures to help you.

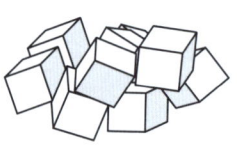   

........ugar   ma........ine   bru........   ....elter

3 Complete the sentences below using the correct words from the box.

shower / chower   chef / shef   presshure / pressure

Caleb is a .... at a famous restaurant.

The .... is broken, so you can't use it.

The team was under .... to score a goal.

Section 14 — Confusing Words

The 'ay' sound

The 'ay' sound can be spelt in lots of different ways.

p**ai**n   spr**ay**   bl**a**d**e**   sl**eigh**   r**ei**n   gr**ey**

1) Draw lines to match each word to the correct pair of <u>missing letters</u>.

anyw**?**   l**?**out   av**?**lable

ay   **ai**   **ey**

Each word contains the 'ay' sound.

expl**?**n   birthd**?**   ob**?**

2) Underline the <u>word</u> in each sentence that contains an '<u>ay</u>' <u>sound</u>.

Yusef decided to decorate the living room.

I heard the horse neighing in the field.

My grandma has lots of beige clothes.

3) Complete each word with the correct spelling of the '<u>ay</u>' sound. Use the clues to help you.

to fill with air → | i | n | f | l | | t | |

the number after seven → | | | | | t |

a mark that won't wash off → | s | t | | | n |

Section 14 — Confusing Words

Plurals

Most plurals are made by adding **s** or **es**.

lion → lion**s**   torch → torch**es**

For most words that end in **f**, change the **f** to a **v** and add **es**.

shelf → shel**ves**

For most words that end in **y**, change the **y** to **ies**.

lady → lad**ies**

1) Draw lines to match each word to the correct plural ending.

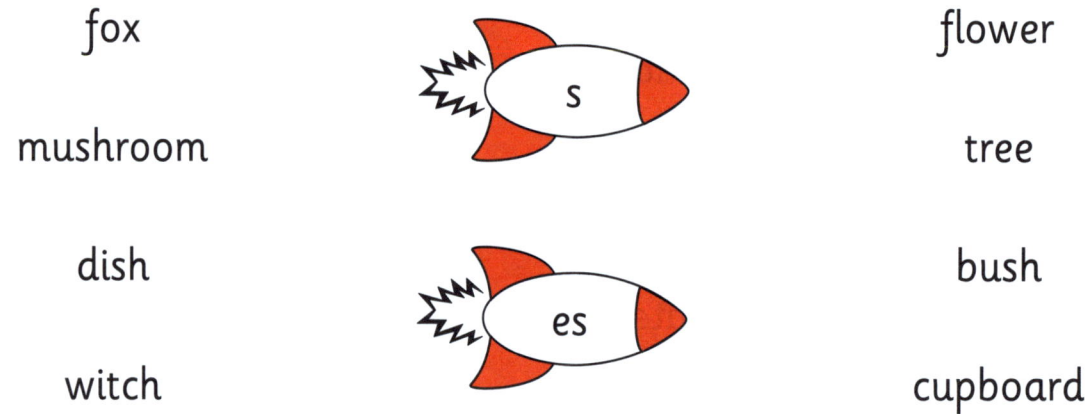

fox		flower
mushroom	**s**	tree
dish		bush
witch	**es**	cupboard

2) Write the plural of each word in the correct box.

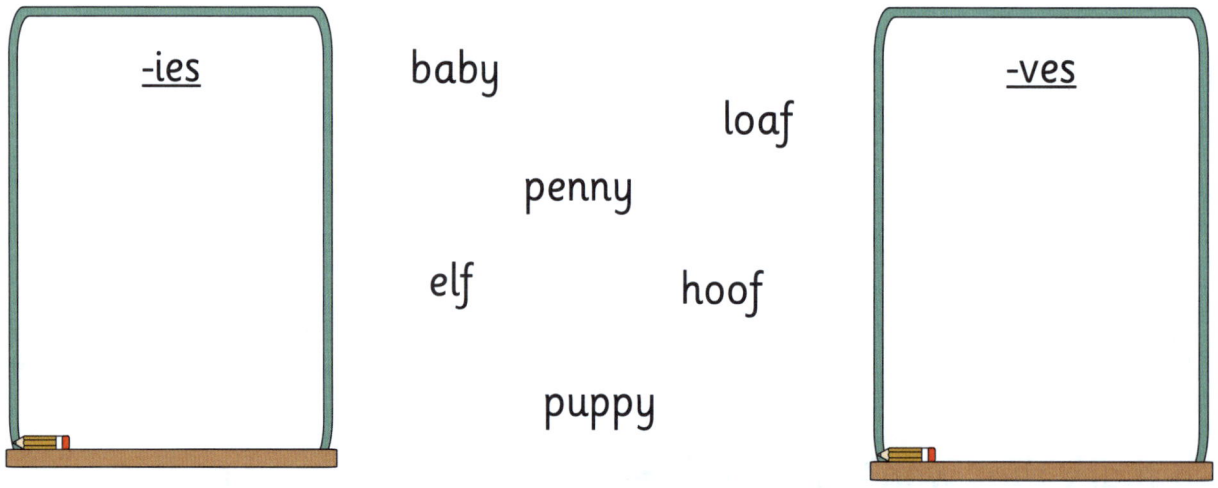

-ies   baby   loaf   penny   elf   hoof   puppy   -ves

Section 14 — Confusing Words   © CGP — not to be photocopied

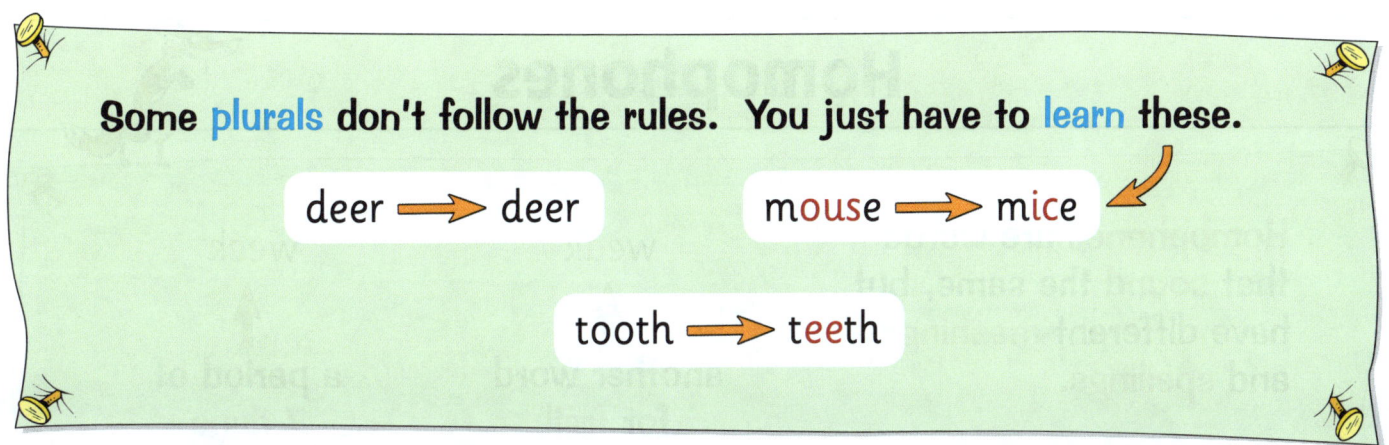

Some plurals don't follow the rules. You just have to learn these.

deer ⟹ deer   mouse ⟹ mice

tooth ⟹ teeth

3) Read each sentence, then write the name of the person who is correct.

Amalia — The plural of woman is womans.

Bushra — The plural of woman is womens.

Suki — The plural of woman is women.

.... is correct.

4) Write the plural of each word on the lines, then find the plural words in the wordsearch.

louse ⟹ lice

foot ⟹ ....

fish ⟹ ....

goose ⟹ ....

person ⟹ ....

R	H	D	L	F	M	N	K	P
G	U	F	I	S	H	A	J	E
A	E	T	C	E	E	F	L	O
I	M	E	E	U	B	E	I	P
V	T	P	S	J	W	E	U	L
B	R	X	H	E	I	T	H	E

5) Complete the sentence with the plural of the word in the box.

child — The teacher told the .... to come inside.

© CGP — not to be photocopied   Section 14 — Confusing Words

Homophones

Homophones are words that sound the same, but have different meanings and spellings.

weak ↑ another word for frail

week ↑ a period of 7 days

1) Draw lines to <u>match</u> each word to the correct <u>picture</u>.

pair
pear

night
knight

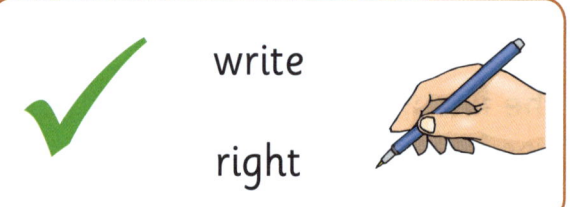

write
right

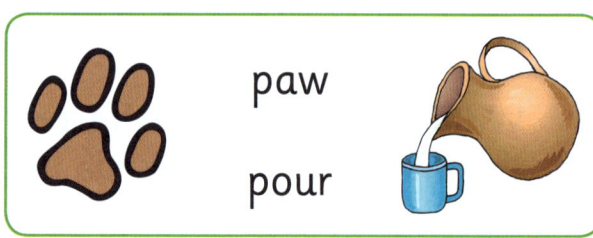

paw
pour

2) Unscramble the letters to find a <u>homophone</u> of the words below. The <u>first</u> and <u>last</u> letters are in the correct places.

g s e u e s d   guest ➡ ....

h r a e d   herd ➡ ....

k w n o s   nose ➡ ....

Section 14 — Confusing Words

3 Draw lines to match each word to its meaning.

a noise a bird makes

to rule as king or queen

not expensive

a type of weather

4 Tick the sentences that use the correct spelling of the underlined word.

I like to <u>reed</u> books and paint pictures. ☐

Tiffany added lots of tomato <u>sauce</u> to her chips. ☐

The children weren't <u>allowed</u> to go out at night. ☐

I have never <u>bean</u> to the theatre before. ☐

5 Circle the correct word to complete each sentence.

Jerome <u>war</u> / <u>wore</u> his smartest shoes to the party.

I put two slices of <u>bread</u> / <u>bred</u> in the toaster.

My sister brushed my <u>hair</u> / <u>hare</u> for me.

I warmed my <u>feat</u> / <u>feet</u> by the fire.

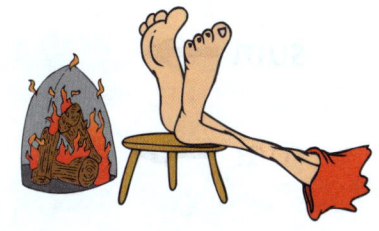

The bird <u>made</u> / <u>maid</u> a nest in the tree.

Section 14 — Confusing Words

6 Complete each sentence with the correct word from the boxes.

| flew   flu |

When I had the ...., I had to stay in bed.

The flock of birds .... off into the distance.

| plane   plain |

The .... couldn't take off because of the snow.

Pierre thought the chef's food was too ....

7 Find a homophone for each of the words below, then find it in the wordsearch.

I'll → isle

sail → ....

berry → ....

wear → ....

sum → ....

roar → ....

```
W K R A W O L H G
H J Y E P I M C Y
E O V I S A R U U
R G H L O D Y K S
E N E X F V E I A
T P O I S H W V L
A U D F G O A X E
Q I B U R Y M P F
Z C T V K A X E N
```

Section 14 — Confusing Words

Glossary

Adjective — A word that describes a noun, e.g. **floppy** ears.

Adverb — A word that describes a verb, e.g. sneeze **loudly**.

Adverbial — A group of words that behaves like an **adverb**.

Article — The words **a**, **an** and **the**.

Clause — Part of a sentence that contains a **subject** (**someone** or **something** doing the action) and a **verb**.

Conjunction — A word or phrase that **joins** two parts of a sentence, e.g. We could visit the museum <u>or</u> we could stay at home.

Fronted adverbial — An **adverbial** that comes at the **start** of a sentence, e.g. <u>At the beach</u>, I built a sandcastle.

Homophones — Words that sound the same but have a different **spelling** and **meaning**.

Main clause — A clause that **makes sense** on its own, e.g. <u>I am angry</u> because you stole my sweets.

Noun — A word that **names** something, e.g. **June**, **rabbit**, **sock**.

Paragraph — Used to **group** related sentences **together**.

Phrase — A group of words usually without a **verb**.

Prefix — Letters that can be put **in front** of a word to change its **meaning**, e.g. <u>re</u>do.

Glossary

Preposition — Tells you **where**, **when** or **why** something happens.

Pronoun — A word used to **replace** a **noun**, e.g. **you**, **we**, **they**.

Subordinate clause — A clause that **doesn't make sense** on its own, e.g. I want to be a firefighter <u>when I am older</u>.

Suffix — Letters that can be put **after** a word to change its **meaning**, e.g. small<u>er</u>.

Verb — A doing or being word, e.g. **eat**, **sleep**, **walk**, **am**.

COMMON PUNCTUATION MARKS

Apostrophes — show **missing letters** and **possession**.	'
Capital letters — used for **starting** sentences and for **names** or **I**.	A
Commas — used in **lists**, to **join clauses** and after some **adverbial phrases**.	,
Exclamation marks — show **strong emotions** or **commands**.	!
Full stops — show where **sentences end**.	.
Inverted commas — show when someone is **speaking**.	" "
Question marks — used at the **end** of questions.	?

Answers

Grammar

Section 1 – Word Types

Page 4 – Nouns

1. You should have ticked: a slippery fish, after dinner, perfect pizza.
2. Common nouns: pumpkin, goats, football
   Proper nouns: Bristol, January, Salima

Page 5 – Adjectives

1. Adjectives: spooky, exciting, interesting, dangerous
2. Any suitable adjective.
   Examples:
   the **slimy** snail
   the **smelly** bin
   the **shiny** ring

Page 6 – Verbs

1. Verbs: pray, learn, speak, write, see
2. He **grows** potatoes.
   We **eat** pancakes.
   It **walks** slowly.
   I **sleep** peacefully.

Page 7 – Adverbs

1. How: quietly, nicely, greedily, sneakily
   When: later, today, now
   How often: always, sometimes, regularly, never
2. The farmer shook his fist **angrily** at us.
   I **usually** eat my dinner at 5 o'clock.
   Diego is going to Spain **tomorrow**.

Pages 8 and 9 – Pronouns

1. **They** sing.
   It rings.
   She looks.
   He plays.
2. When Owais walks to school, Mia walks with **him**.
   The trainers were smelly, so Anthony put **them** outside.
   My rabbits love cabbage, but **they** don't like lettuce.
   Kiah and I were well-behaved, so **we** got a treat.
3. You should have circled: Erika.
   You should have circled: the ducks.
4. The builders made a fence. **They** were proud of it.
   I baked a cake for my sister. She liked **it**.

Pages 10 and 11 – Articles

1. an: apple, onion, aeroplane, exam
   a: dancer, painting, toy, bridge
2. The fireworks scared my dog.
   I am making an omelette for dinner.
   Freya took a photograph of our house.
   I live in the house next door.
3. The chicken laid **an** egg in the hay.
   I stopped to smell **the** purple flower.
   He got **a** bicycle for Christmas.
4. I can't believe we saw an **otter** at the park.
   The **boat** was painted blue.
   Zara asked for a **jigsaw** for her birthday.
5. You should have ticked:
   Reece was going on a journey.
   The cat chased a mouse around the house.
   Lindsay found an olive on her pizza.
   You should have crossed:
   I would like an burger for tea.
   You should have written the sentence:
   I would like a burger for tea.

Section 2 – Clauses and Phrases

Pages 12 to 14 – Clauses

1. main clause: the phone rang, I called them, Abel hid, Annie won
   subordinate clause: unless he's busy, which was red, who was tall, if we can
2. You should have ticked these sentences:
   Ali won the contest while Edie came third.
   We shared an ice lolly before we went home.
3. You should have matched these clauses:
   I love art lessons — because I like using clay.
   Let's play a board game — before we watch TV.
   Erin was my best friend — until she moved away.
   I will wear my red hat — unless I find my blue one.
4. I won't remember the address if I don't write it down. — **subordinate clause**
   Although he was tired, he finished his homework before bed. — **subordinate clause**
   As the alarm didn't go off, they are running late for school. — **main clause**
   We should go home before we get into trouble. — **main clause**
   She wants a job building robots when she is older. — **subordinate clause**

Answers

5. Meera ate the crisps <u>even though she wasn't hungry</u>.
   <u>Although it was late</u>, Andy couldn't fall asleep.
   <u>When I am older</u>, I want to be a ballet dancer.
   Tyler likes his new house <u>because it has a garden</u>.

6. You should have ticked these subordinate clauses:
   unless you are quiet
   because I hate heights
   although it might rain
   You should have made these sentences:
   Unless you are quiet, you'll scare the animals.
   Although it might rain, I want to go for a walk.
   I don't like flying **because I hate heights**.

7. Any suitable sentence which includes a main clause.
   Example:
   When it was hungry, **the bird ate a worm**.

Page 15 – Phrases

1. Phrases: in the attic, perhaps later, despite the warning, really excited, bright red bus

2. Delilah sang **like an angel**.
   Abdul ran **really fast**.
   Snakes are **dry and scaly**.
   The owl hooted **at midnight**.

Pages 16 and 17 – Noun Phrases

1. You should have ticked these phrases:
   the steep red slide
   an orange goldfish
   crushed ice
   purple and yellow flowers
   my favourite book

2. Noun phrases: red light, tall giraffes, bitter dark chocolate, the roaring lion, bright green ball, sparkly purple unicorn

3. a crowd of **excited** people
   the **yellow** car in the driveway
   a cup of **tasty** hot chocolate
   the young girl **in** the photo
   the blue scarf **with** the red spots
   the room **on** the second floor

4. Any suitable noun phrases.
   Examples:
   the **scared** cat with **the green eyes**
   the **orange** cat with **a red flower**

Section 3 – Adverbial Phrases

Pages 18 and 19 – Adverbial Phrases

1. You should have circled the following adverbial phrases and written them on the board:
   quite carefully, very happily, too quietly, so badly, really slowly

2. You should have matched these pairs:
   The couple were talking — extremely loudly.
   I coloured the picture — almost perfectly.
   They stroked the puppy — very gently.

3. They are setting up a stage in the square. — **where**
   We all met up in York two weeks ago. — **when**
   Roy and Tabitha always help out at home. — **where**
   Fabian's knee started to hurt after the match. — **when**

4. Aisha trains with her team **every Saturday**.
   I always wake up for a drink **during the night**.
   We fed the horses **at the farm**.
   Jack won the race **quite easily**.

Pages 20 and 21 – Fronted Adverbials

1. You should have ticked these sentences:
   Before bed he drank a glass of milk.
   In front of the building there is a statue.
   Very quietly they left the house.

2. My dad is going back to work next month. — **End**
   As quickly as possible, they ran away. — **Start**
   They packed their bags in a hurry. — **End**
   In four months, my sister will start school. — **Start**
   I found my ring on top of the fridge. — **End**
   From the window, I saw my rabbit escaping. — **Start**

3. You should have ticked these sentences:
   Under the sea, there are lots of different fish.
   Over the hill, there is another town.

4. You should have written these sentences:
   By the library, I bumped into my friend.
   In the meadow, there were lots of flowers.
   Next June, Chris is going to a concert.

5. Any suitable answer.
   Example:
   On her skateboard, she moves quickly.

Answers

Section 4 – Conjunctions and Prepositions

Pages 22 and 23 – Conjunctions

1. You should have circled: nor, yet, for, or.
2. Gopal wasn't feeling well, **so** he stayed at home.
   She made me a present, **and** she got me a card.
   They were going to sit outside, **but** it started to rain.
3. Wasim was upset **because** he'd lost his scarf.
   After I finished painting, I washed my hands.
   It was midnight **when** I heard the owl hoot.
   Drink some water **if** you are thirsty.
4. Put your gloves on **before** your hands get cold.
   I waited outside **while** he packed his bags.
   She told us off **after** we stole her biscuits.

Pages 24 and 25 – Prepositions

1. Any suitable answers.
   Examples:
   The books are **on** the shelf.
   The sugar is **next to** the mug.
2. There are lots of photos in this magazine. — **where**
   I went to Kendra's house after school. — **when**
   He saw the deer near the old mill. — **where**
   The foal hid behind its mother. — **where**
   The work has to be finished by tomorrow. — **when**
   I haven't seen him since last week. — **when**
3. You should have ticked these sentences:
   The plane flew above the clouds.
   The children had to be home before teatime.
4. I was having fun **on** the slide.
   Let's put the flowers **in** a vase.
   The horse galloped **around** the field.
   She won't answer her phone **before** 8 o'clock.
5. The boy is **in front of** the bench.
   The bird is sitting **on** the bench.
   The bucket is **next to** the bench.
   The sandals are **under** the bench.
   The ball is **in** the boy's hands.

Section 5 – Verb Tenses

Pages 26 and 27 – Present Tense and Past Tense

1. simple past: smiled, wanted, jumped, skipped
   simple present: scratch, shout, throw, hug
2.

Simple Present Tense	Simple Past Tense
I wait outside.	I **waited** outside.
He **talks** to the postman.	He talked to the postman.
She hates peas.	She **hated** peas.
They **laugh** at the clown.	They laughed at the clown.
We relax at home.	We **relaxed** at home.

3. You should have shaded: swam, asked, bit, kissed
4. They **paid** for everyone's meal.
   I **buy** toy models of trains.
   Sami saw a mouse and **screamed** loudly.
   Yesterday, I **watched** cricket with Shaun.
   Carly **scores** all the goals for her team.
   We **take** the bus to school.

Page 28 – Using 'ing' verbs in the Present

1. She **is writing** a story.
   They **are having** a race.
   He **is cooking** burgers.
2. He **is dancing**.
   We **are jogging**.
   She **is waiting**.

Page 29 – Using 'ing' verbs in the Past

1. You should have ticked:
   We were cleaning.
   He was acting.
   She was knitting.
   I was training.
2. Beth **was sobbing**.
   John **was smiling**.
   The twins **were shouting**.

Pages 30 and 31 – The Present Perfect

1. present perfect:
   The door has closed.
   We have wasted time.
   I have signed up.
   He has washed up.

Answers

2. She **has smashed** the mirror.
   We **have spotted** a fox.
   He **has boiled** the kettle.
   They **have won** the match.

3. You should have ticked:
   He has failed his test.
   It has started raining.
   They have fixed it.
   He has ripped the paper.

4. I **have driven** to work today.
   My plants **have grown** lots.
   He **has taken** lots of photos.
   Fadila **has spoken** to her teacher.

5. My cat **has stolen** the food.

Pages 32 and 33 – Staying in the Same Tense

1. You should have matched these phrases:
   We are running. — They are walking.
   I have looked. — She has hidden.
   He was dancing. — She was singing.

2. You should have ticked:
   I bought a pizza, and then I ate it for dinner.
   Patrick is washing the plates and he is dusting the shelves.
   We play loud music and dance around the living room.

3. Richard caught a cold, so he **stayed** at home.
   We are baking a cake because we are **having** a party.
   On Sundays, I see my sister, and we **play** tennis.

4. You should have drawn lines to make these sentences:
   Jill waited patiently — while Ria brushed her teeth.
   Jill waits patiently — while Ria brushes her teeth.
   Jill is waiting patiently — while Ria is brushing her teeth.

5. I bought a boat and **sailed** it on the lake.
   They play cricket when it **is** sunny.
   Rajan **watched** TV before he went to bed.

6. I used a pencil because **I lost** my pen.
   Bai runs up the pitch and scores a goal.

Section 6 – Standard and Non-Standard English

Pages 34 and 35 – Verb Agreement

1. I **am** looking for my rucksack.
   She **is** listening to pop music.
   We **are** talking about holidays.
   They **are** watching cartoons.

2. You should have ticked these sentences:
   I am looking forward to the party.
   Everyone knows what happened.

3. You should have drawn lines to make these sentences:
   My parents have — gone to Paris.
   Last year, my parents — went to Paris.
   At the cinema, Carrie — ate all the popcorn.
   Carrie has already — eaten all the popcorn.

4. Lucas and I **went** to the zoo with some friends.
   Put your hand up if you haven't **done** the homework.
   Dad **did** the washing, and he helped Mum make dinner.
   My cousins have **been** to Ireland recently.

Pages 36 to 38 – Confusing Words

1. **Petra** used pronouns correctly in their sentence.

2. He doesn't want to speak to **them**.
   We should ask **them** what they want.
   These cupcakes are revolting.
   I saw **them** steal the apples.
   Why don't you like **these** shoes?

3. You should have matched these pairs:
   I would of liked to come. — I would have liked to come.
   He could of helped us. — He could have helped us.
   I should not of done it. — I should not have done it.
   You would of been bored. — You would have been bored.

4. We would **have** been happy to see you.
   Melissa and **I** sit next to each other.
   My neighbour's dog has never liked **me**.
   There's a box **of** chocolates on the kitchen table.

Answers

5. Standard English:
    Nobody could have predicted it.
    I decided to take an umbrella.
    Non-Standard English:
    They told me about them bullies.
    Pablo and me made daisy chains.

6. You should have shaded in this sentence:
    I wear these boots in winter.

7. Those yoghurts are mine, but **these** yoghurts are yours.
    I wish I could **have** seen the shooting star.
    My cousin asked **me** to help her make a cake.

Page 39 – Negatives

1. Standard English:
    I spoke to <u>nobody</u>.
    There were <u>none</u> left.
    Non-Standard English:
    They <u>didn't</u> do <u>nothing</u> wrong.

2. There wasn't **anybody** there.
    We didn't have **anywhere** to sit.
    He doesn't have **anything** to say.
    I told you I haven't got **any**.

Punctuation

Section 7 – Sentence Punctuation

Pages 40 and 41 – Capital Letters and Full Stops

1. Capital letter: scotland, thursday, amy, london
    Lower-case letter: week, dinner, horse, shirt

2. My cousin, jane, has moved house.
    — **Capital Letter**
    I accidentally got on the wrong bus — **Full Stop**
    We painted our living room yellow — **Full Stop**
    i didn't want to go to the park. — **Capital Letter**

3. My sister Anya and I are going shopping. We are catching a train from the station. I'm looking for some glittery shoes, and Anya wants to buy a stripy dress.

4. Yesterday I visited my **friend.**
    My brother lives near **Manchester.**
    We went to the park in the morning.
    I watched the rugby match.
    Today I played with my friend **Daisy.**
    There's lots to do **where** they live.

5. You should have written these sentences:
    My dog is called **B**arry.
    Sue doesn't like **F**ridays.
    We are visiting **F**rance.

Page 42 – Question Marks

1. What time is the next ferry arriving**?**
    We ate all of the cake before the party**.**
    Where did you go on Sunday**?**

2. You should have circled: Who, What, When
    What is your friend's name?
    Who left the door open?
    When can I go outside?

3. Any sensible sentence which starts with a capital letter and ends with a question mark.
    Example:
    Where are you going on holiday?

Page 43 – Exclamation Marks

1. Watch out for that **shark!**
    I am peeling **potatoes.**
    That **thunder** was terrifying**!**
    She is going to **bed.**

2. **I scored the winning goal!**

Pages 44 and 45 – Sentence Practice

1. There's a lion over there!
    Who is she?
    Where is the shop?
    I actually scored a goal!
    I'm so late for school!
    What's happening?
    When is the meeting?

2. Yesterday, I saw a dog wearing a **mask!**
    Lilith's favourite **hobby** is rowing.
    How many slices of **pizza** would you like**?**

3.
!	?
That's great	How is the pie
Ouch, my toe	Why is it dark
Wow, how fun	Who are you

4. You should have ticked:
    I forgot Ishana's birthday!
    Kit is swimming across the English Channel!
    Broccoli is a green vegetable.
    You should have written these sentences:
    Where can **I** buy some new shoes**?**
    How many days are in **July?**

Answers

Section 8 – Commas

Pages 46 and 47 – Commas for Writing Lists

1. You should have ticked these sentences:
   Have you got any apples, bananas or grapes?
   The dog chased a bird, a squirrel, a cat and some cows.
   You should have put a cross next to these sentences:
   Have you got any apples bananas, or grapes?
   The dog, chased a bird, a squirrel, a cat and some cows.

2. The jelly could be orange, lemon or lime flavour.
   Gina's brothers are called Aidan, Stephen and Jake.
   The journey was long, boring and tiring.
   Mix the sugar, butter and eggs together.

3. His mum bakes cookies, bread and cakes. — 1
   We saw seals, dolphins, sharks and whales. — 2
   I like peas, potatoes, cabbage and sprouts. — 2

4. I'm going to invite Mandy, Imran and Sadie.
   The house was small, dusty and haunted.
   The mouse ate the cheese, the crackers and the cherries.

5. Any suitable answer using commas between the first three items but not the last two.
   Example:
   I lost my **old brown boots, new rucksack, silver house key and blue woolly hat.**

Pages 48 and 49 – Commas to Separate Clauses

1. You should have ticked these sentences:
   While he was sitting outside Theo got sunburnt.
   If it's raining we won't go to the beach.
   Before it went dark Nancy went out for a walk.

2. Before we forget, let's write it down.
   Wherever she went, she was admired.
   Even if it's true, I don't believe it.
   Because of the snow, the race was cancelled.

3. **Nikolas** and **Rifa** used commas correctly.

4. You should have circled the commas in these sentences:
   I took it downstairs, because I wanted to open it.
   I wasn't sure, whether I should tell anyone about it.

5. If I have time, I want to visit Grandma.

Pages 50 and 51 – Comma Practice

1. The fruit was shiny, juicy and tasty.
   — **to separate items in a list**
   If I'm late, my aunt tells me off.
   — **to separate clauses**
   As he ran away, they shouted at him.
   — **to separate clauses**
   I have a rubber, a pen and a pencil.
   — **to separate items in a list**

2. You should have ticked these sentences:
   We ordered a burger, some chips and a drink.
   Catalina waited outside until they had left.
   While I'm in town, I will do some shopping.

3. I went to the pet shop to buy a collar, a lead, a food bowl and some chew toys.
   The caretaker asked his boss for a new mop, a bigger bucket, a better broom and a cup of tea.

4. You should have added commas to these sentences:
   If you're lucky, you might see a deer.
   Even though he was tired, he kept running.
   You should have shaded the circle next to this sentence:
   She couldn't go because she had to work.

5. Any suitable answer using commas between the first three items but not the last two.
   Example:
   I put **a lamp, the gloves, my sunglasses and some bananas** on the table.

Section 9 – Apostrophes

Pages 52 and 53 – Apostrophes for Missing Letters

1. You should have shaded: she'd, you've, I'd, we'll

2. **where's**
   that'll
   didn't
   I've

3. You should have ticked:
   I wasn't ready for school.
   We've been skiing.
   They're meeting soon.
   You should have written out these words correctly: **He's**, **You'll**, **We'd**

4. **Sophie's** skipping.
   They're melting.
   It's a pencil.

Answers

5. My dad thought that **he'd** won the lottery.
   Ingrid doesn't eat eggs because **she's** allergic to them.
   I miss my brothers now that **they've** moved out.

Pages 54 and 55 – Its and It's

1. The tree lost its leaves. — **Belonging to it**
   It's the third time! — **It is**
   It's been a long day. — **It has**

2. You should have underlined the 'its' in these sentences:
   Its scary — it has red eyes and sharp teeth.
   I don't want to go because its been snowing.
   Its been in the oven for too long.

3. **It's** Friday night.
   It's really unfair.
   It's having a nap.
   Its name is Sam.
   It's chilly today.
   Its ears are pointy.

4. There's an owl. It's got wings. — **it has**
   This is so fun. It's great. — **it is**
   I think it's too scary for me. — **it is**
   Look at the mess it's made. — **it has**

5. I'm going for a walk because **it's** a nice day.
   I baked a cake and **it's** turned out well.
   I can't ride my bike because **its** tyre is flat.

Pages 56 and 57 – Apostrophes for Single Possession

1. **Daria's** bag, **Rhys's** ball, **Jelani's** boot, **Lewis's** book

2. You should have ticked:
   My watch's battery died.
   Alena's shoes are pink.

3. I borrowed Deandre's coat.
   We were amazed by the zebra's stripes.
   Rosie was the ship's captain.
   It is Marvin's turn to roll the dice.

4. The bus has wheels. They are the **bus's wheels**.
   The hen has a nest. It is the **hen's nest**.
   The fire has sparks. They are the **fire's sparks**.
   The cactus has spikes. They are the **cactus's spikes**.

Pages 58 and 59 – Apostrophe Practice

1. Missing letter:
   Wow, it's spicy!
   He's laughing loudly.
   Sorry, I'll be late.
   We're landing soon.
   To show possession:
   Chris's feet are huge.
   The shirt's pockets.
   Find Leo's trainers.
   It is Sakura's toy.

2. You should have ticked:
   I peeped into the rhino's enclosure.
   The telephone's buttons were broken.

3.
it is	it has
It's too early.	It's bitten me!
It's February.	It's been hard.
It's funny.	It's taken ages.

4. I **can't** believe it.
   They're very pleased.
   I'm shorter than her.

5. Any sentence which uses apostrophes correctly.
   Example:
   The dog stole the man's sausages.

Section 10 – Inverted Commas

Pages 60 and 61 – Punctuating Speech

1. You should have circled the inverted commas in bold:
   "It's very rainy today," said **"**Mrs Griffin.
   "Tori is my **"**best friend," said Isaac.
   "I want pizza for dinner," said Chang**"**.
   "I don't like maths," **"**said Beatrice.
   "We're**"** having fish for dinner," said Lesley.

2. You should have ticked:
   "My favourite sport is hockey," said Acacia.
   "My dog is called Boris," said Fred.
   Latoya said, "I'll play outside today."

3. Comma: "It's my birthday today**,**" said Ava.
            Paco said**,** "I can play guitar."
   Full Stop: Kieran said, "My birthday is in July**.**"
            "My dad plays the drums," said Emilia**.**

4. Lani said**,** "I want to be a doctor when I grow up."
   "London is my favourite place to visit**,**" said Oliver**.**

5. Nick said, **"G**rape juice is my favourite drink.**"**

Answers

Pages 62 and 63 – Punctuating Speech with ! or ?

1. Exclamation mark:
   "Come here now**!**" shouted Toby.
   Paul shouted, "This is the best day**!**"
   Question mark:
   Rania said, "Can you turn the light on**?**"
   "When is your party**?**" asked Maylin.

2. You should have ticked these sentences:
   Jashan asked, "Why can't I go to Thea's house?"
   "How are you today?" asked Laszlo.
   "Don't eat chocolate before dinner!" she cried.

3. You should have circled the words in bold:
   Matthew asked, "**please** can I have some more?"
   "**get** away from the fireplace!" the woman yelled.
   Yara shouted, "**the** zoo is amazing!"
   "**ready** or not, here I come!" Ethan shouted.

4. "What time do the shops open**?**" asked Karl.
   "Football is great**!**" yelled Amir.
   The girl asked**,** "Can you pass the salt?"
   "I can't hear you!" shouted Penelope**.**
   "Where is Sabrina today**?**" asked Mr Wilson.

5. You should have inserted the following inverted commas and circled the lower-case letters in bold. You should have matched the sentences to the following capital letters:
   Kinga thought, "**w**hich colours should I use?" — W
   "**m**y team is better than yours," I shouted. — M
   The alien said, "**t**ake me to your leader." — T

Section 11 – Paragraphs and Layout

Pages 64 to 66 – Paragraphs

1. You should have shaded:
   When you're writing about a different time.
   When you're writing about a new person or subject.
   When you're writing about a new place.

2. You should have matched these sentences:
   Jonah's father is a baker. — He makes pastries.
   I speak German at home. — My mum is from Berlin.
   Amna can't run today. — She has broken her foot.
   They hated English. — They preferred maths.

3. person
   time

4. new person

5. You should have added these paragraph markers:
   Rajesh's birthday is in August. He likes having his birthday in August because he doesn't have to go to school. // In July, Rajesh started planning his birthday party. He hoped his parents would let him have a fancy-dress party like his sister. // "You're not allowed to copy me!" shouted his sister. He always copied her ideas and she was tired of it.
   You should have circled these reasons:
   2nd paragraph — New time
   3rd paragraph — New person speaks

6. **Christmas was Charlie's favourite time of the year. He loved eating all the food.**
   　"I hope Dad makes mince pies," he said.

Page 67 – Headings and Subheadings

1. You should have put the boxes in this order:
   2 — The dog that rescued a cat.
   3 — Seb the dog was on his morning walk when he heard cries coming from a well. He looked inside and saw his neighbour's cat, Tilly. Luckily, the well wasn't deep, so he managed to pull Tilly out.
   1 — FRIENDS OR ENEMIES?

2. BEST HOLIDAY IDEAS — **Heading**
   Paris — **Subheading**
   London — **Subheading**

Spelling

Section 12 – Prefixes

Pages 68 and 69 – Prefixes – 'dis' and 'mis'

1. You should have matched:
   disagree — to not agree with something
   mishear — to not hear something correctly
   misunderstand — to not understand correctly
   displease — to not please someone

2. dislike — **dis** + **like**
   mismatch — **mis** + **match**
   misinform — **mis** + **inform**
   disorder — **dis** + **order**

3. You should have shaded: misbehave, dishonest, mistreat, disallow.

Answers

4. dis-: approve, appoint, similar
   mis-: spell, shape
   You should have written the following words:
   disapprove
   misspell
   misshape
   disappoint
   dissimilar
5. They **misprinted** Della's picture in the book.
   "Class **dismissed**," said the teacher.

Pages 70 and 71 – Prefixes – 'in', 'il', 'im' and 'ir'

1. **illegal**
   irrelevant
   invisible
   impolite
2. You should have ticked: mobile, mortal, pure
   You should have written:
   immobile
   immortal
   impure
3. You should have circled: secure, valid, formal, expensive
   You should have written:
   insecure
   invalid
   informal
   inexpensive
4. I have an **irrational** fear of butterflies.
   Eating dessert first is **illogical**.
   The shape was **irregular**.
   Someone who can't read is **illiterate**.
5. **incapable**
   impossible
   illegible

Pages 72 and 73 – Prefixes – 're', 'anti' and 'auto'

1. re-: action, send, open, view
   anti-: climax, clockwise
   You should have written:
   reaction
   anticlimax
   resend
   anticlockwise
   reopen
   review
2. You should have circled: graph, pilot.
   You should have written:
   autograph
   autopilot
3. You should have shaded:
   re — **fresh**
   anti — **bacterial**
   auto — **correct**
4. The magician made the missing rabbit **re**appear.
   Dr Williams started to write his **auto**biography.
   She put some **anti**septic cream on my finger.
5. **anti**social
   replay
   automobile

Pages 74 and 75 – Prefixes – 'sub', 'super' and 'inter'

1. sub-: **submerge**, **subtotal**
   inter-: **intercity**, **interact**
2. **superhero**
   supermarket
3. The **sub**way goes under the main road.
   The museum has an **inter**active dinosaur exhibit.
   Everyone wanted an autograph from the **super**star.
   A really big shop is called a **super**store.
4.

			¹s					
			u					
			p					
			e				³s	
²i	n	t	e	r	n	e	t	u
			p					p
			o					e
			w					r
⁴s| u	b	h	e	a	d	i	n	g
			r					l
								u
⁵s	u	b	m	a	r	i	n	e

Answers

Section 13 – Suffixes and Word Endings

Pages 76 and 77 – Suffixes – Double Letters

1. You should have matched:
   grinn — **ing**
   soon — **er**
   regrett — **ing**
   sharp — **er**
   cancell — **ing**
   You should have written:
   grinning, sooner, regretting, sharper, cancelling

2. You should have ticked: shop, slip, prefer, chat, spot, drum.

3. **t — hotter**
   n — planned
   p — popping

4. You should have circled: tripped, singing, lower, upper, swimming.

5. The run**ner** approached the track.
   The rabbit was hop**ping** across the field.
   Mary jab**bed** her brother with a pencil.

Pages 78 and 79 – Suffixes – 'ation' and 'ous'

1. Scotland is a very mountain**ous** country.
   Many species of frog are poison**ous**.
   Elliot needed rest and relax**ation**.
   Rosa Parks was very courage**ous**.
   My bananas are grown on a plant**ation**.

2. She tried to find the treasure's **location**.
   Peter made **preparations** for the journey.
   Not wearing a seatbelt is **dangerous**.
   Ayo made a **donation** to a local charity.

3. **adoration**
   nervous
   invitation

4. Changed: **sensation, creation, decoration**
   Unchanged: **expectation, formation, information**

5. You should have ticked: joyous, continuous, hazardous.
   You should have crossed:
   fameous, outragous, ridiculeous
   You should have written:
   famous, outrageous, ridiculous

Pages 80 and 81 – Suffixes – 'ly'

1. complete → completely — **doesn't change**
   gentle → gently — **changes**
   angry → angrily — **changes**
   whole → wholly — **changes**
   near → nearly — **doesn't change**

2. **deadly**
   actually
   likely

3. exact — exactly
   quick — quickly
   glad — gladly
   quiet — quietly

4. July was **slightly** cooler than June.
   The shop **normally** opened at nine o'clock.
   Savannah climbed the mountain **easily**.

5.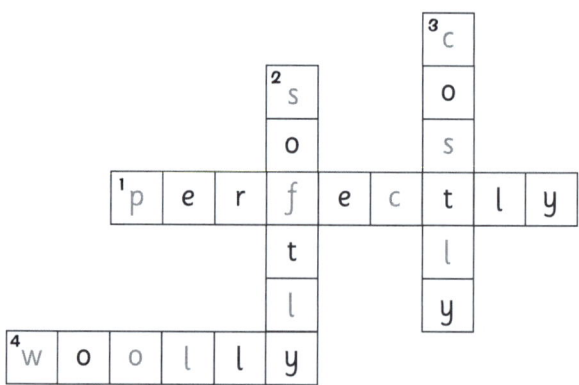

Pages 82 and 83 – Word Endings – 'sure' and 'ture'

1. -ture: **gesture, mixture, torture, adventure**
   -sure: **enclosure, pressure, leisure**

2. There was a lot of **moisture** in the air.
   "It's my **pleasure** to be here," he said.
   A factory was built to **manufacture** cars.
   The **creature** growled as I approached the cage.

3. t**r**easure
   n**ature**
   f**u**rniture

4. ture — literature
   sure — measure
   ture — structure

5. Thermometers record the tempera**ture** of something.
   The clo**sure** of the village shop angered the locals.
   My grandpa loves making minia**ture** models of ships.

Answers

Pages 84 and 85 – Word Endings – the 'shun' sound

1. You should have ticked: location, politician, suggestion.
   You should have crossed: accian, invencian, electrition.
   You should have written:
   action, **invention**, **electrician**
2. The doctor gave the baby her **injection**.
   The **magician** turned the prince into a frog.
   Gloria went to the **optician** for an eye test.
3. permi — ssion
   explo — sion
   discu — ssion
   inva — sion
   expre — ssion
   -sion: **explosion**, **invasion**
   -ssion: **permission**, **discussion**, **expression**
4. The mathemati**cian** is great with numbers. She is especially good at divi**sion** and can find a solu**tion** to any maths problem. She runs a weekly se**ssion** at her local school.

Pages 86 and 87 – Word Endings – 'gue' and 'que'

1. You should have shaded: zigzag, plague, league, strong, gong, meringue
2. She looked through the cata**logue** for a new fridge.
   The birds started to sing their morning son**g**.
   The boy's ton**gue** got stuck to his ice lolly.
3. d**ialogue**
4. pla — que
   bouti — que
   ban — k
   tas — k
   grotes — que
   mos — que
5. The tiger **stalked** its prey.
   They tried to learn the **technique**.
   The lizard **basked** in the sun.
   She took a **chunk** of cheese.
   I brought two **flasks** of tea.
6. an**tique**

Section 14 – Confusing Words

Page 88 – The short 'i' sound

1. You should have circled: bliss, ginger, tiptoe, Egypt, list.
2. 'i': s**i**ster, l**i**zard, v**i**ctory, b**i**tter, s**i**gnal
   'y': p**y**ramid, m**y**stery, s**y**stem
3. The astronaut hoped to **discover** a new planet.
   I rode my **bicycle** to school on Monday.

Page 89 – The short 'u' sound

1. My **brother** plays basketball.
   These **gloves** belong to Nala.
   The car was old and **rusty**.
2. m**o**ney, f**u**nfair, tr**ou**ble
3. M**o**nday, th**u**nder

Page 90 – The hard 'c' sound

1. book, talking, picnic
2. **c**amping, s**k**ater, an**ch**or, unlo**ck**

Page 91 – The soft 'c' sound

1. You should have shaded: century, fleece, pace, police, peace, concert.
2. **Gethin** has spelt the underlined word correctly.
3. Nobody in the offi**c**e ate any cake.
   Lina collected the par**c**el on her way home.
   I used some **sc**issors to cut out the shapes.

Page 92 – The 'sh' sound

1. You should have shaded: finish, tissue, shiver.
2. **s**ugar, ma**ch**ine, bru**sh**, **sh**elter
3. Caleb is a **chef** at a famous restaurant.
   The **shower** is broken, so you can't use it.
   The team was under **pressure** to score a goal.

Page 93 – The 'ay' sound

1. 'ay': anyw**ay**, l**ay**out, birthd**ay**
   'ai': av**ai**lable, expl**ai**n
   'ey': ob**ey**
2. Yusef decided to decorate the living room.
   I heard the horse neighing in the field.
   My grandma has lots of beige clothes.
3. infl**a**te, **eigh**t, st**ai**n

Answers

Pages 94 and 95 – Plurals

1. 's': mushroom, flower, tree, cupboard
   'es': fox, dish, witch, bush
2. 'ies': **babies**, **pennies**, **puppies**
   'ves': **loaves**, **elves**, **hooves**
3. **Suki** is correct.
4. **feet**, **fish**, **geese**, **people**

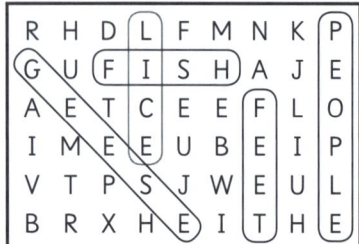

5. The teacher told the **children** to come inside.

Pages 96 to 98 – Homophones

1. You should have matched the words to these pictures:

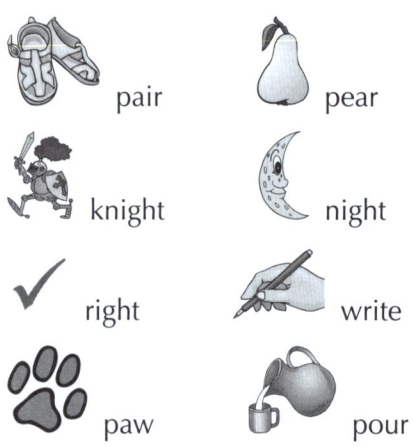

pair, pear, knight, night, right, write, paw, pour

2. **guessed**, **heard**, **knows**
3. You should have matched these pairs:
   rain — a type of weather
   reign — to rule as king or queen
   cheap — not expensive
   cheep — a noise a bird makes
4. You should have ticked these sentences:
   Tiffany added lots of tomato sauce to her chips.
   The children weren't allowed to go out at night.
5. Jerome **wore** his smartest shoes to the party.
   I put two slices of **bread** in the toaster.
   My sister brushed my **hair** for me.
   I warmed my **feet** by the fire.
   The bird **made** a nest in the tree.
6. When I had the **flu**, I had to stay in bed.
   The flock of birds **flew** off into the distance.
   The **plane** couldn't take off because of the snow.
   Pierre thought the chef's food was too **plain**.
7. **sale**, **bury**, **where**, **some**, **raw**

```
W K R A W O L H G
H J Y E P I M C Y
E O V I S A R U U
R G H L O D Y K S
E N E X F V E I A
T P O I S H W V L
A U D F G O A X E
Q I B U R Y M P F
Z C T V K A X E N
```